W9-CAI-640

OVERLOOK ILLUSTRATED LIVES:

Henry James

Mary Ann Caws is Distinguished Professor of English,
French, and Comparative Literature at the Graduate School
of the City University of New York. She is the author of
many books, including two additional titles in the Overlook
Illustrated Lives series, Virginia Woolf and Marcel Proust.
She lives in New York.

Henry James

Mary Ann Caws

OVERLOOK DUCKWORTH

NEW YORK • WOODSTOCK • LONDON

B
JAmes

T4473

First published in the United States in 2006 by
The Overlook Press, Peter Mayer Publishers, Inc.
Woodstock, New York, and London

NEW YORK:
141 Wooster Street
New York, NY 10012

WOODSTOCK:
One Overlook Drive
Woodstock, NY 12498
www.overlookpress.com
[For individual orders, bulk and special sales, contact our Woodstock office]

LONDON:
Gerald Duckworth & Co. Ltd.
Greenhill House
90-93 Cowcross Street
London EC1M 6BF
www.ducknet.co.uk

Cataloging-in-Publication Data is available from the Library of Congress

Type formatting and layout by Bernard Schleifer Company
Printed in Singapore
ISBN-10 1-58567-543-1   ISBN-13 978-1-58567-543-2 (US)
ISBN10 0-7156-3638-3   ISBN-13 978- 0-7156-3638-1 (UK)
9 8 7 6 5 4 3 2 1

10/05/07 $19.95

Contents

Acknowledgments

My warmest thanks to all who helped with the information for this small volume, in particular to Dawn An, Rachel Brownstein, Dana Milstein, Sarah Bird Wright and R. Lewis Wright, and to the archivists and curators at Art Resource, New York City; the Beinecke Library, Yale University; the Century Association, New York City; the Picture Collection, New York Public Library; Houghton Library, Harvard University. Special thanks to my editors at The Overlook Press, David Mulrooney and David Shoemaker, and to my agent, Katherine Fausset at Curtis Brown, Ltd.

Seeing in Henry James

What an intensely visual writer was Henry James. Desiring to
be appropriate to his own lifelong attachment to scenes in his
writing, he enters his notebooks: (on Dec. 21, 1896): "I realise—
none too soon—that the *scenic* method is my absolute, my imper-
ative, my *only* salvation" (N, 167). This brief illustrated life means
to concentrate not on the chronological narration so completely
and accurately laid down by Leon Edel, R.L.B. Lewis, Fred Kaplan,
and reflected upon recently by Colm Toíbín and David Lodge, but
rather on the more vivid moments of telling, of friendships, of
places, illuminating the events of James's writings. This small
story wants to tell not about the worlds of journalism, travel writing, drama, or serious publishing that were, naturally, all-impor-
tant in James's experience, but about places, pictures, and people
frequented by the Master.

Reading James is likely to provoke, if not irritation, then deep
enthusiasm. He says of himself that he was "a man of imagination at the active pitch" (Auto, 199) to such an extent that it is a
matter of "keeping his abundance down." (Auto, 156) The over-
abundance of James which he strives to "keep down" may well
become the readers' own. One antidote may be an irony sensed in
the slightest and the greatest of the Master's own lessons—like
the famous "Lesson of the Master" about preferring writing to living, betrayed by the Master in that story, who himself marries and
"lives." In his Notebooks, James had noted down an interesting
situation: an elder artist or writer, ruined by his marriage, pro-
duces cheap works with rapidity . . . befriends a younger confrere
whom "he sees on the brink of the same disaster and whom he
endeavours to save." (N, 43)

Cynthia Ozick's hilarious and poignant story of herself and James tells it wonderfully. Young, she was thinking herself into him: (Ozick, 294) "When I say I 'became' Henry James, you must understand this: though I was a near-sighted twenty-two-year-old young woman infected with the commonplace intention of writing a novel, I was *also* the elderly bald-headed Henry James. Even without close examination, you could see the light glancing off my pate; you could see my heavy chin, my watch chain, my walking stick, my tender paunch." Then, of course, she figured out that the Master had been saying at her age, and was still saying now, through the famous outcry of Strether in *The Ambassadors*: "Live, live!" And that the true lesson was—is— "never to venerate what is complete, burnished, whole, in its grand organized flowering or finish . . . never to worship ripe Art or the ripened artist; but instead to seek to be young while young, primitive while primitive, ungainly when ungainly—to look for crudeness and rudeness, to husband one's own stupidity or ungenius." (Ozick, 296)

For years, Henry James was to me—and for so many others of us aware of our own "ungenius"—a genius of a writer, a master of narration, an object of near to humorless reverence. The Master, the Master. I would repeat with that same reverence his three commandments, going something like this: "The first is, be kind. The second is, be kind. And the third, be kind."

My reverence hasn't lessened. But the aim of writing a brief sketch of his life has lightened some of its gravity. All of a sudden, various odd details, some comic, some baroque, some just plain creepily Jamesian appeared to dart across the once so determinedly solemn canvas. And the details seemed of themselves living, in their very randomness, and perhaps each of them a clue to something not always stressed in James's own recounting or in others' recounting of his being.

How about going out on the Venice Canal to dispose of the black gowns of a deaf woman writer who has jumped from a window probably in despair over your inability to devote yourself to her, and seeing them rise up billowing with air over the water, all around you? How about one of your favorite actresses, starring in your illfated play *Guy Domville*, Elizabeth Robins, finding that George Parkes, to whom she had been married, had used the stage armor he always kept in his closet to drown himself in the Charles River (Edel 4, 36)?

Henry James

As for style, how about calling a volume of your writings "Terminations" and another, "Embarrassments." Melancholy, to be sure, but self-consciously placed in evidence as if in irony: with James, of course, we often don't know. How about writing to your gardenlady, (Ed3 106) Miss Muir Mackenzie, about Mrs. Paddington, the housekeeper you are meeting for the first time: "She is my Fate! May she not be my Doom," and then greeting Mrs. Paddington with the cheery message: "I have come to meet my doom"?

And of course, his own reputation for unununderstandability soared with the years, and the jokes associated with it, such as the lady who boasted she could read Henry James "in the original." Or another who knew "several languages, French, New Thought, and Henry James." Indeed. Irresistible. Thus this illustrated life of James.

Mrs. William James, Mary Margaret James, William James and Henry James, in Cambridge, 1904

James Country

but so small is this neat little world of ours
—Alice James, Diary, January 27, 1891 (162)

"He needs no other assigned place," said William of his younger brother, "than his family heritage." When Henry had taken up residence abroad, (362) William wrote to his wife: "He's really, I won't say a Yankee, but a native of the James family, and has no other country." But "For Henry, the country for which he had left America was not England, but art." In the intense land that was the James family, everything was reflected upon, enormously, given (Auto, 34) "the quantity of our inward life" in his father's house. The family was deeply part of a Boston/Cambridge New England community. Emerson introduced them to Margaret Fuller and Thoreau, and they all introduced each other to current ideas. Henry's two grandmothers already gave them opposite ways of looking at things. (N, 10) One Presbyterian, conservative, Scottish and Scots-Irish, living at no. 19 Washington Square in New York, and the other, in Albany, liberal, republican and Anglo-Irish.

Brothers and sister: to Henry, William always seemed superior, and remained his hero, despite the immense contrast in their personalities and minds and writings. Little Alice was five, Wilky, in all his "pudgy sociality," and the "impulsive" Bob,

Ralph Waldo Emerson, c. 1870

who went away to fight for the Union side in the war which both he and Wilky joined, and in which Wilky was gravely wounded.

What a family. Henry Senior had had his dramatic incident, when, in an outdoor chemistry experiment, turpentine was splashed over the thirteen-year old Henry's pants, and when a balloon entered a hayloft in a stable nearby and was about to set the whole thing afire, Henry ran in, climbed to the loft and stamped out the fire. But in so doing, he set his own flesh on fire, so that his leg had to be amputated beneath the knee. (K, 13) Later, Henry the junior was to worry whether his father's lameness might have been connected to his lack of literary success. Henry Senior had also had his vision. In 1844, he suffered a sort of nightmare, in which a menacing form crouched before him, to his utter panic. He then chose as his religion that of Swedenborg, an 18th century Swedish mystic. This was already marginal behaviour, but in his extreme individualism, he even refused to join the Swedenborgian church (21): attending none, one was of course accepted in all. He reasoned: "there was no communion . . . from which we need find ourselves excluded." The famous joke about his writing on *The Secret of Swedenborg,* in 1869, was that told by William Dean Howells: "He kept it." (85)

Henry James Jr. hated being "Jr," and went about unacknowledging it, signing H. James for a while,

Right: *Henry James, Sr., c. 1880*

Below: *William Dean Howells, with daughter Mildred. 1898.*

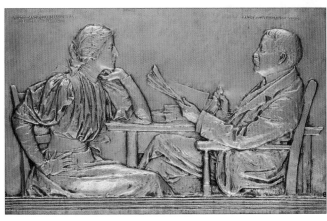

until, in 1882 at his father's death, the "Jr. " was no longer appropriate. But both the hallucinations and the father's wound, were passed on in a sense, to his family. William saw black shapes, Henry at age 12 was "appalled" by a mysterious figure he saw in the Galerie d'Apollon in the Louvre, and whom he pursued: a family of visionaries, clearly. And when Henry was pushed into a corner, and sprained his back, he had a wound like his father, to which he would refer always as his "obscure hurt." It was not what we would think of as a calm family.

Henry had sailed for Europe the first time in 1843, with his family and Aunt Kate, from which time dates his first memory, that of wiggling his feet under a flowing robe, and seeing from his carriage the column of the place Vendôme, the Napoleon memorial, in 1844. When, at the end of his life,

Right: *Henry James, Sr. and Henry James, Jr., c. 1830*

Below: *Galerie d'Apollon.*

Above: The Vendôme Column, c. 1870

Below: *Théodore Géricault*, The Raft of the Medusa, 1819

he entered into a Napoleonic fantasy, he was rounding out the circle.

The James tribe seemed, for a long time, to live on both sides of the ocean: in Cambridge and Boston, but also in London, Geneva, and Paris, as well as Boulogne-sur-Mer. There were so many migrations that telling some of them only, as Henry did, must have seemed to be enough. It seems next to unbelievable. By the time William was 13, he and Henry together had attended at least 10 different schools. (LM, 93)

Above: William James, at 19

Again in 1855, they made their way back to Europe from New York, landing at Liverpool and going to London straightaway. In Paris this time, James was struck by the drama of Géricault's *Raft of the Medusa,* in all its "splendour and terror of interest". (27) Stage drama was no less riveting. After a time in Geneva (where William was in school, but Henry was sick with malaria), they went to London for the winter. Here, Henry was able to admire Charles Kean (son of the great actor) in Shakespeare, Alred Wigan in French melodrama, and Charles Mathews in a Sheridan play. So many returns: in 1856, they returned to Paris, and wandered about, changing habitations three times. From the rue de Seine to the Luxembourg Palace, everything beckoned with a vivid impression that would

Below: Charles Kean

Above: *View of Boulogne*

Below: *William James in Geneva, 1859-60*

never lessen for the author, who remembered nostalgically, "Such a stretch of perspective, *such* an intensity of tone as it offered in those days." (30) They went to Boulogne-sur-Mer for the summer, back to Paris in the fall, and in December back to Boulogne-sur-Mer, on the rue Neuve Chaussée. This return is omitted in Henry's autobiography, as is one of the returns to Newport. It does seems a bit restless, this moving about, and somewhat embarrassing.

Suddenly, in the summer of 1858, William declared that it was painting which most interested him, and after three years in Europe, they returned to Newport, so that William could study with William Morris Hunt and John LaFarge. Back they went to Geneva in fall, where Henry went to almost the least likely school, the polytechnic. Then, in 1860 Henry Sr. determined the boys should learn German (a language he did not know), so they went to Bonn. But by September, they were back in Newport. Eventually, William attended Union College in Schenectady, and gambled. The father, of course, expected his son to do honor to his name. He himself had attended, left, returned and graduated 1830, and then set off for England and Ireland, with his black servant and friend Joseph Henry.

John La Farge, Peacocks and Peonies I, *1882*

Henry Jr. never spent a day in college, only in Harvard Law School, in 1862, which turned out to be a mistake: he lasted a year. He joined William in a Cambridge boarding house, then moved to Winthrop Square. In 1864, the family moved from Newport to Boston, to live on Ashburton Place, then to Cambridge, where they lived at 20 Quincy Street, until Henry and Mary James died, both in 1882. They had done so much moving, from house to hotel to pension to apartment, in so many countries, that settling was finally the most intelligent move.

Mary James, c. 1875

Growing up, and later, Mary James had been the central figure in Henry's life. After her death, and after dining in the family home on Quincy Street, he walked back to Boston "in the clear American starlight, along those dark damp roads, where, in the winter air, one met nothing but the coloured lamps and the far-heard jingle of the Cambridge horse-cars." It was an oddly harmonious time. "Mother's death appeared to have left behind it a soft benefi- cent hush in which we lived for weeks, for months, and which was full of rest."

The relation between the brothers is as intrigu- ing to the reader as to the historian, and to the various interpreters of the James country. In

William James in the Garden at Lamb House, Rye, East Sussex, 1908

March of 1910, William and Alice came over to Rye, and in late June, Henry and William went to Switzerland, hoping it would be good for William, ill as he was. But he worsened, and returned then to Chocorua, in the barn William had bought in 1886, to Chocorua Lake, near Conway, five hours from Boston. Henry went to be with him when he was dying. At William's death, Henry greatly mourned "my protector, my backer, my authority and my pride." (531) William had asked his younger brother to remain for six weeks in Cambridge after his death to see if he could communicate with him past the grave. (LM, 435) Henry returned to England in July of 1911, but we don't have any record of the success of that postmortal venture. But the relation of the two brothers has given rise to much speculation, which attaches also to some of the odd crossdressing stories Henry wrote: for example "The Death of the Lion," in which the characters have cross-gendered names and beings, and (K, 91) the odd tale of "Certain Old Clothes," full of brotherhood, sisterhood, marriage and intermarriage, death, and garments, one sister being killed when she tries to wear her dead sister's dress. All very odd doings, in James country.

But James had several countries, and two languages. From his many stays in France, and from his early home tutoring with French governesses, Henry acquired a command of French constantly surprising to the unsuspecting reader. He wrote his French friends in flawless French, held his own in French communities of writers, like the salons of Gustave Flaubert on Sundays, and easily conversed with Turgenev, who knew only Russian and French.

Portrait of Ivan Turgenev, Illya Repin

Left: Henry James, March 1890

Right: Henry James, 1906

Always, Henry was aware of his own privileged situation, itself responsible for that very "being apart" feeling he was destined to have. (167) "[H]is own separateness was complete, inviolate," and, during the First World War, looking at and after the soldiers wounded, he realized how far they were from his own situation, the son of Henry James Senior, kept far from the battle lines. His entire life, with its patches of solitude and of sociability—he said he dined out during the 1878-8 season between 107 and 140 times (depending on his conversation)—he was to savor, (172) as deeply as he could, this quiet and strange treachery, his own surreptitious withdrawal from the world."

His memories themselves quiver with intensity, like the feeling he depicted himself as always seeking: (17) "just to be somewhere. . . and somehow . . . feel a vibration." Always he felt himself straining to be an individual self, so surrounded by selves he saw as stronger. One of the glories of London was that eccentricity was warmly welcomed. The self-reflections in his autobiography portray him as both separate and sensuous, from the sight of the Vendôme Column, through the detailed memory of fresh peaches in Albany by the bushel: "peaches big and peaches small, peaches white and peaches yellow. . . . Above all the public heaps of them, the high-piled receptacles at every

Henry James in London

turn, touched the street as with a sort of southern plenty . . ."(A5, 42). He remembers living at 11 Fifth Avenue, remembers (A58) "the small warm dusky homogeneous New York world of the mid-century," (9) the Hudson River Railroad, and Broadway stretching out, and incarnating all "the joy and adventure of one's childhood . . . prodigiously, from Union Sq to Barnum's great American Museum by the City Hall," and remembers particularly (48) burying his nose in a book to sniff the paper and ink, "the English smell" they called it. Everything seemed alive, insistent, alert. His return visits to New York were no less permeated with the delight in the everyday life of a big city. In 1875, he spent a winter in New York, arriving in January at No. 111 East Twenty-Fifth street, where the streets were unpaved and the sight of the 2nd Avenue El showed its "fantastic skeleton."(Ed2, 184)

England he loved right off and always. His first glance of Cambridge, as he looked across Christ Church meadow, was ecstatic: "hundreds of the mighty lads of England, clad in white flannel and blue, immense, fair-haired, magnificent in their youths, lounging down the stream in their punts or pulling in straining crews and rejoicing in their godlike strength." The famously golden youth Rupert Brooke punted Henry James down the river, an event Henry never forgot. Playing cricket, punting, crewing, and just being, the young men satisfied something in Henry James of the same sublimity as the "Great serene tower" of Magdalen College.

London became his life, together with Lamb House in Rye (which he deeply loved, with sunlight striking the old brick wall, and his garden room to write in: "Only Lamb House is mild; only Lamb House is sane; only Lamb House is true." (1900), p. 100.)

It was graced with eight writing tables, one of which he could give to visitors like his brother. In the winter, he wrote mostly in the upstairs green room, and in warm weather, in the detached garden house. He would dictate there from 10 am to 1:45, pacing up and down, making very few revisions in the beginning, then many more. When, in 1896, James developed a pain in his wrist, he had engaged a stenographer, the silent Scot William MacAlpine, the first in a trinity of stenographers—who, at first, made drafts for him, which he would read over and alter. When he began to dictate, pacing up and

Henry James in the Garden at Lamb House, c. 1900

Henry James at his desk in the Garden House

Henry James at Lamb House

down, his style would become noticeably more involved, his sentences more complicated.

His writing habits did not change. He would dictate in the morning, the time when he always wrote, and then in the afternoon, take a walk or a ride with MacAlpine, for whom he had purchased a bicycle. Eventually, MacAlpine (hired elsewhere, more lucratively) was replaced by Mary Weld—"the little Weldina," a definite jewel, responsible for typing the last part of The Ambassadors, and all of The Wings of the Dove and The Golden Bowl, as well as the biography of Story and many of the tales, including "The Beast in the Jungle"—and finally, in 1907, by Theodora Bosanquet, also a writer.

Finally, he had to leave Lamb House and its damp chill for the comfort of the city. There he lived in many places: from

a hotel in Trafalgar Square, to an apartment Charles Eliot Norton found him in 1869, on Half Moon Street, off Piccadilly, from Tite Street in Chelsea (near Whistler's home, in which the painter Sargent then lived), to De Vere Gardens. Having lived all over in England for forty years, remarkably, at the end of his life, with the onset of the war, he was counted an alien. At that point, he decided to become British, with Edmond Gosse as his witness and sponsor.

Henry was never to forget his European experience, recreating, it, returning to America, but finally settling abroad, as a "passionate pilgrim" taking a position away, removed, always away from his home port. From a negative point of view, this may have seemed a self-condemnation to live only "in a world of acquaintances," to leave behind one's country, as an accusation sometimes went. Indeed, solitude seemed often to set in, and discouragement. But carrying with him that James country, James was finally—I think— at home in himself.

De Vere Gardens, London

Above: *Henry and William James in Rye, 1901*

Left: *Henry James in Rome, 1899*

A Double Consciousness

> *in arranging and fitting yourself here, you have always to remember and count with the far-backness in which the simplest evolution retroacts, and in the manner of doing, the rigidity imposed by the long burden of Time, whilst in Yankeedom it is simply tomorrow that you must stretch yourself to.*
> —*Diary of Alice James, March 23, 1891 (182)*

Always, from almost the beginning, Henry James was gifted with a consciousness of a double nationhood. The family, of course, shuttled back and forth from Europe to Massachusetts and New York— and the very richness of such a non-narrow point of view endowed him with the truest kind of liberal thinking. Later on, clearly, he took as his intended stage for writing and realization the doubleness of place. The American abroad, of course, ambassadorially as in the novel of that name, but also a refusal of being tied down to any one way of conceiving life. "I aspire to write in such a way that it would be impossible to an outsider to say whether I am, at a given moment, an American writing about England or an Englishman writing about America . . . far from being ashamed of such an ambiguity I should be exceedingly proud of it, for it would be highly civilized." (Edel 2, 391) Part of his lifelong struggle with his older brother William the philosopher had this origin, and just as equally vice versa—opposed to the practical and pragmatic way of being and writing, Henry felt a rejection from this side of America.

As for his attachment to Europe, it took many forms, and for a while mostly concerned France or Italy. With his friend Sarge Perry, he "had agreed that literature at its most valuable and rich and intense was written in the countries which Napoleon had reigned over and attacked; literature lay in the places where Roman coins could be found in the soil." (Letters, 241)

The single consciousness of which he was so desperately aware after his return in 1870 to no. 20, Quincy Street in Cambridge, with his parents, William and Alice, after fifteen months in the old world. It made him feel cramped, as if he was suddenly reduced "now after the campaniles and cathedrals, the glimpses of pagan and Papal Rome, the theatres of Paris, the studios of the pre-Raphaelites." (Edel 2, 19) To him now the rustic, detached houses of Cambridge, this twenty-two-year attempt to mix old and new was "a terribly comfortless business." Such was always his view, even upon his return for a year in the United States in 1904-5. Europe and England, were engraved forever in his soul. Yet, there was a time for travel writing, and it was not to be forever. He should now make more notes of travel, joining with others: "the *keen* love and observation of the picturesque is ebbing away from me as I grow older, and I doubt whether, a year or two hence, I shall have it in me to describe houses and mountains, or even cathedrals and pictures." (Edel 2, 129)

Henry James. Pencil sketch by John Singer Sargent, 1894

Vernon Lee
[Violet Paget] *by John
Singer Sargent, 1881*

In Paris, and then in London, he had his habits. Parisian, he would write in the morning, walk in the afternoon, dine out in the evenings, preferring his rare roast beef *(rosbif saignant)* and English ale. He was the very opposite of the American abroad whom he saw Hawthorne to be, making his way through churches and galleries, too shy to respond to paintings and sculpture as a traveler from a simpler civilization. Simpler: James was rarely that.

James was satirized in a story called "Lady Tal" by "Vernon Lee," in her story collection *Vanitas.* She pictured him as having expatriated himself, and being thus forced to live "in a world of acquaintances." Although he often criticized his younger brother, particularly for his lack of obvious plot lines and difficult dialogues, William very much disliked others to criticize him (or of course anyone in the family, that James nation.) So he felt his

desire for a visit with the bluestocking author "quenched," as he put it, upon reading the story. (Edel 3, 560)

The always "life-loving, life-searching" James wanted above all else to keep up his intensity of vision and writing, and finally found London the best place of all, deciding to live there: "with the bond of our glorious tongue . . . how great is the great city which we may unite fraternally to regard as the capital of our race" (English Hours, 22). Leon Edel calls the years between 1870 and 1881 "The conquest of London." For ten of his most profitable years, he lived in London, at 3 Bolton street, just off Piccadilly, on the eastern verge of Mayfair, two floors up. Even when it was disagreeable, mournful, and the rest, it was for him "only magnificent . . . The most complete compendium of the world." There, he always felt like an old inhabitant. "The weather is hideous, the heavens being perpetually ensatined with a crust of dirty fog-paste, like Thames mud in solution. At 11 am I have to light my candles to read! . . . however indeed, in spite of fog & isolation & a very dreary Xmas, I rejoice in all things & find that I have the making of a good Londoner." (Edel 3, 353) Now this was not the same as being an Englishman, until, in the last year of his life, he actually became one, his principal sponsor being Edmond Gosse. What he

William James, 1907

remained was (Edel 2, 278) an "observant stranger . . . I am not at all Anglicized, but I am thoroughly Londonized— a very different thing." He writes of this in an essay of 1888: "We are far from liking London well enough till we like its defects: the dense darkness of much of its winter, the soot on the chimney-pots and everywhere else, the early lamplight, the brown blur of the houses, the splashing of hansoms in Oxford Street or the Strand on December afternoons." (English Hours, 19)

How he became Londonian is the way many of us become Jamesian, by listening. What he heard was the chatter of the streets and the sidewalks and their figures, the cobbles and the carts, "so many sermons of the very stones of London." He had, he said, "to improvise a local medium and to arrange a local consciousness." (Auto, 565) Now this local consciousness was the very opposite of the one cultivated in New England, and in fact, in James's novel *The American,* the New England minister Babcock seems, to the critic Sheldon Nozick, a mirror image of William, who will leave when the character representing Henry speaks of his love. (Nozick, 288) Love of persons, of place: the theme reappears in *The Ambassadors*, when a New Englander, Strether, is sent over to Paris to rescue for America the young man Chad, who has been waylaid by the wiles of Paris and Parisians, such as

Garden at 110 rue du Bac, *William Glackens, 1929*

the lovely Madame de Vionnet. But, notably, it is here in this
novel, in the garden of the painter Gloriani, that the injunction will
be issued: "Live, live all you can. It's a mistake not to." The interi-
or garden of the American painter James Abbott McNeill Whistler
at 110 rue du Bac is supposed to be that place in which this
injunction is issued, as it were, by proxy, for once in Torquay
James had heard the tale of William Dean Howells saying to
Jonathan Sturges in that garden that one should "live all one
can," about which then James wrote at length in his notebook.
James had visited Whistler there, and in 1875-6 had seen the garden on his visit to the house overlooking it, talking with a friend
of Fanny Kemble—his great actress, who was often in motion,
like Henry James, traveling between her house in Germantown,
Pennsylvania, and London, Switzerland, and Italy—who dressed in
lavender velvet and Venetian lace, was the epitome of grandeur, of
"human largeness" and was all the more attractive for her hoarse
speaking voice. (Edel 2, 352). Madame Mohl, who herself had
been a friend of Madame Récamier and Chateaubriand, was an

example of French history and literature intermingling, as always. On the morning of February 25, 1897, when James was lunching in De Vere Gardens, with Conrad, James had written to Whistler, "with the artist, the artist communicates." (ED5,51) So they did. And that communication was about living through art.

Italy, Spain, France—returning to Europe after America was returning to a kind of deep experience much valued by the artistic temperament. Writing to Grace Norton about Rome—Grace with whose husband Charles Eliot Norton, sixteen years older than himself, James had traveled in Europe, "But I found myself, *with* him, Methusalesque and alien!"—James remarks that Rome is "interesting . . . thoroughly serious . . . a depth of tone which makes it differ not only in degree but even in kind, from Florence & Venice." James exults, travelling from London to Paris: "Dear People all! I take possession of the old world! I inhale it! I appropriate it!" And again, on Oct. 20, 1881, having visited at Quincy Street, and then staying at the Brunswick Hotel in Boston, he exclaims: "My choice is the old world, my choice, my need, my life." (Letters, 315). One can't get much clearer than that.

Torquay

Boston Commons

The chasm between the old style of Europe and the largeness and loudness of America is a constant—"how greasily-greenback much of American life must look to you in your retrospect. I don't know what is to become of us—We're too big & booming & brassy to live." (Letters, 242, to Dr. William Wilberforce Baldwin, 19 Oct 9) Not that James's innocent characters traveling abroad are loud and large—but their very innocence can be a large irritation. Take Daisy Miller. Take Strether. They learn, perhaps, yet do not shriek their lesson from the rooftops. The vivid impressions James is able to give have often to do with the double nature of his consciousness, bridging Europe and America: "I had also looked at France and looked at Europe, looked even at America as Europe itself might be conceived to look." (Auto, 199)

Some of James's recountings stick in the mind: what he loves he describes with zeal and unforgettable radiance of detail. His

Italian adventures remain unforgettable for the reader, Florence in the winter light: (Nozick, 230) "It was so bright and yet so sad, so still and yet so charged, to the supersensuous ear, with the murmur of an extinguished life, that you could only say it was intensely and adorably strange." Near the Spanish steps, he would stop at the Caffe Greco, for an ice or a glass of beer.

Not far from Florence, in Bellosguardo, James spent time with William and Emelyn Story, in their rooms high up in the Palazzo Barberini, on the slope of the Quirinal. The left wing of the Palazzo was a gallery, Cardinal Barberini's apartment was on the ground floor, and a steep stair in the right wing led to the William Wetmore Story's apartment, consisting of 50 rooms on upper stories. There James met many from the artistic world, including Matthew Arnold. The sculptor Story figures in Hawthorne's *Marble Faun*, a tale otherwise known as *Transformation,* and James, strenuously invited by the family to write Story's story, felt he had to do so. Story's studio in the Via San Nicola da Tolentino had many plaster casts on view, and there, his figures were draped in sweeping and sensuous cloths.

Alice, dying for so long a time, was the opposite of sensuous. Always she seemed to be ill, and, at the end of her life, when Katherine Loring was so willing to take care of her and when James was as attentive as ever, she moved to Argyle Road. Now in Constance Fenimore Woolson's novel *Horace Chase*, an invalid sister plays a bigger and bigger role in the heroine's life. It could be suggested, and has been, that at Alice's death, Constance might have found James closer to her, sisterless as he was. (Edel 3, 317) Alas. To be continued.

Unsurprisingly, given his temperament, Venice was the city close to James's heart. In 1869, Alice and Aunt Kate and he, after a bout of traveling had spent four days in Venice, taking gondolas about, visiting the island of Torcello, eating figs, and generally escaping the fierce heat by spending time on the water and in the cool old churches. (Edel 2,74) "The mere use of one's eyes, in

Above: Piazza San Marco, Venice

Left: No. 4161 Riva degli Scaglioni, Venice

Below: Plaque at Riva degli Scaglioni

RIVA
SCHIAVONI

Venice, is happiness enough." It had always been that way for him, as for travellers and dwellers always. Venice, as he put it, was a "refuge of endless strange secrets, broken fortunes and wounded hearts." (Venice, 41)

There, in 1881, he took furnished rooms four flights up, at No. 4161 Riva degli Schiavoni, just across from "the great pink mass of San Giorgio Maggiore." His 1907 preface to *The Portrait of a Lady* recalls his rooms on the Riva Schiavoni: "the waterside life, the wondrous lagoon spread before me, and the ceaseless human chatter of Venice came in at my windows. . . ." And again, as he was finishing his novel, he looked out over "the far-shining lagoons, the pink walls of San Giorgio, the downward curve of the Riva, the distant islands, the movement of the quay, the gondolas in profile." (Edel 2, 439) Now James had his habits: taking his morning coffee at Florian's, then taking a gondola to the bathhouse Stabilimiento Chitarin for a heated saltwater bath, then a walk until his breakfast at Gran Caffé Quadri, then working until six, "and then going back to Florian's after dinner."

Above: Florian, Venice

Below: Gran Caffé Quadri, Venice

Florian's was founded in 1720, as "Venezia Trionfante" (Venice Triumphant), by Floriano Francesconi, then refurbished in 1859 with many separate intimate spaces, spaces once frequented by Rousseau, Goethe, and Byron. The Quadri, was itself once frequented by Stendhal, Balzac, and Proust. (It lost some of its appeal when the occupying Austrians too to hanging out there). James was, on both sides of the piazza, part of a long writers' tradition.

In Venice, he rarely felt alone. There was always company in the drawing room of Katherine De Kay Bronson, in her palazzo the Casa Alvisi, at the mouth of the Grand Canal, opposite from the church Santa Maria della Salute. In her circle, which included Robert Browning, James met the American couple Daniel and Ariane Curtis, who were to be his lifelong friends.

Mr. Curtis had, alas, once tweaked the nose of an aristocratic friend, been jailed, and gone bitter about America—so they purchased the Palazzo Barbaro, just across from the Accadémia, in 1885. In their absence, James would occupy it, finding it "cool, melancholy, empty, delicious." That very deliciousness of melancholy, however, had, like Venice, its very dark side.

Mrs. Jack—the rich and lonely Isabella Gardner—rented this palazzo when the Curtises went to the Oberammergau to the Passion play, and then a second time. She was exhausting to her friends: "she is not a woman—she is a locomotive with a Pullman car attached," said James. (He made similar remarks on Edith Wharton's frenzied hurtling about.) He describes (Nozick, 126), on July 15, 1895, "the age of Mrs. Jack, the figure of Mrs. Jack, the

Palazzo Barbaro, Venice

American, the nightmare—the individual consciousness—the mad, ghastly climax. . . . The Americans looming up—dim, vast, portentous—in their millions—like gathering waves—the barbarians of the Roman Empire." Above all, she delighted James once by placing him in a bed in the library of the Palazzo Barbaro, when she had rented it from the Curtises. He loved looking up at the ceiling with its arabesques. The very idea of the writer surrounded by books, water, and melancholy, stirs the readerly soul.

Great Friends

Much in James's life was about meeting and introducing, no matter where he was living at the moment. His very social existence was, we might guess, rendered possible by the inward life he had such long practice in maintaining, and by his constant work. When in London, which he loved ("I am not an Englishman, I am a Londonian," he would say, "and a perfect bachelor"), he, like many other Londonians, counted on his club as another home, and—after trying out eight of them—chose the Reform Club as his permanent entertaining place. There he could leave his clothes, and hold his dinner parties, and read his newspapers. Only when it closed in the summer was he obliged to invite his

Reform Club,
London

guests elsewhere. His notebooks are full of dates and guests invited, of travels and people seen.

An American until the last year of his life, James had a great appreciation for a few Americans, such as, of course, his New England friends from always. He would visit the Louvre with the philosopher Emerson and Charles Eliot Norton, the great Dante scholar—at whose house, "Shady Hill," he had experienced a sort of "positive consecration to letters" (Ed 208)—and the editor of the *North American Review.* In James' opinion, Norton "took art too hard and Emerson not hard enough. . . ."(77) Whereas there were, says James, "certain chords in Emerson that did not vibrate at all . . . his presence has a sovereign amenity." When also there were the Lowells, staying in the Hotel Lorraine near the Quai Voltaire, Paris felt like a little Cambridge. Oliver Wendell Holmes's son John was there at one point: "the doctor minus versatility and plus modesty." (76) When there were just the three of them, the friendship deepened: "Emerson waxes unworldly; Norton waxes cold." But Lowell touched Henry deeply by being "the oddest mixture of the loveable and the annoying, the infinitely clever and the unspeakably simple."

During one period in Paris, in 1872, he saw a lot of the philosopher Charles Sanders Pierce, dining with him at least twice a week. Writing home about him, James described him, purplefaced, "trundling on tip-toes along the Boulevard, as he did at home along the Main Street." Since he never seemed to be at anything in particular, it could be assumed, said James, that he was drinking up knowledge from the street. William had figured out the way to be with the philosopher so famous in linguistic and semiotic circles: you should treat him like a nettle, grasping it firmly, as opposed to indulging one's natural awe and even overawe in his presence. (LM, 203)

There were not only New England thinkers around, but others, with different accents and outlooks. Mark Twain was another American who found favor with James: "a fine, soft-fibered little fellow with the perversest twang and drawl, but very human and good." (Ed 3, 393) He found Twain "so exclusively a genius, as

essentially one as a typewriter is a typewriter, I
mean as inapt for anything
out of his particular line as
this machine to boil a
potato. Fortunately his
particular line is immense.
He is very simple, very
married, very babyfied, &
very happy. . . ."

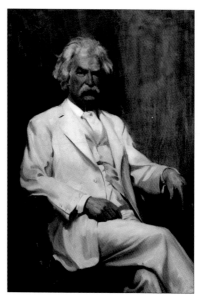

Much that was English
James loved greatly,
including its celebrated
writers. He particularly
loved Leslie Stephen and
his wife Julia Duckworth:
(Edel 3, 153) "she was
beautifully beautiful, and
her beauty and her nature
were all active applied
things, making a great difference for the better for
everybody. Merely not to
see her any more is to have
a pleasure the less in life."
He had visited Stephen at
his house in St. Ives, and
seen the famous lighthouse,
had walked on the moors
with "the silent Stephen,
the almost speechless
Leslie," (K 389) whom he
had found "infinitely
touching and backward-
reaching," but who had—
of all things—introduced

him to the brand-new London Underground. Now Stephen was on his death bed, surrounded by "beautiful ghosts," including his daughters Vanessa and Virginia, who had their mother's beauty.

Another of James's favorite friends was Robert Louis Stevenson, (132) who lived on the brink of a gulley, the Alum Chine, in a yellow brick house with a blue slate roof called Skerryvore, after a lighthouse a Stevenson ancestor had built. He was often clothed in a bohemian velvet jacket. His affection for James was immense, but it has to be admitted that his poems on that subject were a cause for embarrassment to James. In one of these, Stevenson writes how his female characters are so famously attached to their maker:

> Lo, how these fair immaculate women walk
> Behind their jocund maker;
> But he, attended by these shining names,
> Comes (best of all) himself—our welcome James.

On his home ground, near Lamb House—in Winchelsea, not far from Rye were Joseph Conrad and Ford Madox Ford (aka Huefer). In 1901, they often came to visit Lamb House. James, a mature fifty-thre to Conrad's thirty-nine, was troubled by Conrad's morbidity, and temperament. (Edel 3) James wrote generously to the Royal Literary Fund in 1902, to support the grant to Conrad, saying: "the Nigger of the Narcissus is in my opinion the very finest and strongest picture of the sea and sea-life that our language possesses—the masterpiece in a whole great class, and Lord Jim runs it very close . . . when I think that such completeness, such intensity of expression has been arrived at by a man not born to our speech, but who took it up, with singular courage, from necessity and sympathy, and has laboured at it heroically and devotedly, I am equally impressed with the fine persistence and the intrinsic success." James cared intensely, his life long, about the English language, its use and its pronunciation (witness his scathing address to the Bryn Mawr students about the sloppy diction of Americans), and that a Polish-born writer should have been so successful was enormously impressive to him. "His production

Portrait of
Joseph Conrad,
Walter Tittle

has all been fine, rare, &
valid." To Conrad, James
exclaimed: (469) "I read you
as I listen to rare music—with
deepest depths of surrender,
and out of those depths I
emerge slowly and reluctantly
again, to acknowledge that I
return to life . . . You stir me
. . . to amazement and you
touch me to tears."

In another version of his
double consciousness, James
was equally attuned to the
French and the English literary circles. With his frequent
voyaging across the channel, he was a perfect bridge between the
cultures.

About the French, both authors and persons, James was both
admiring and cutting. As he wrote to William (Kaplan, 163) "The
longer I live in France, the better I like the French personally, but
the more convinced I am of their bottomless superficiality . . ."
Not only was James's spoken and written French impeccable, but,
from very early on, he enjoyed translating, starting with Alfred de
Musset's play *Lorenzaccio* and Merimée's *Vénus de L'île*. The
French authors James particularly enjoyed reading and meeting
included Stendhal. On March 25, 1870, he found his *Chartreuse de
Parme* outstanding. "It seems to me stronger and more truthful
than the author's books of profound observation, theory &c. It is
certainly a great novel—great in the facility & freedom with which
it handles characters & passions." He found Taine "remarkably
pleasant—much more bonhomie, mildness and geniality, than his
hard, splendid, intellectual, logical style and manner had led me
to expect. . . ." And, making notes on his experiences in Paris, celebrated, on April 8, 1893, "The strange genius of Pierre Loti—so
exquisite even in a thing so *mince*, so comparatively shrunken and

limited, as *Matelot. . . .*" Marcel Proust
(Nozick, 53, 65)

In Edith Wharton's autobiography *A Backward Glance* (324), she speaks of sending *Swann's Way* to Henry James: "he devoured it in a passion of curiosity and admiration . . . instantly recognized a new mastery, a new vision . . . the encounter gave him his last, and one of his strongest, artistic emotions." Proust, says George Painter in his biography of the writer, received a letter from Henry James "informing him that this was an extraordinary book for so young an author . . . and that it was a great pity he lived in advance of his time." (Tintner, 133, quoting from George Painter: *Proust: The Later Years* Boston, 1965, 252, n. 2)

He had loved *Tartarin de Tarascon,* mostly for Alphonse Daudet, and in fact translated its last volume into English in 1889. On Daudet's very

Portrait of Charles Dickens, W. Warman

Alphonse Daudet and his daughter Edmée, *Eugene Carrière*, 1890

small body—James affectionately called him "the little thing," referring also to Daudet's novel *Le Petit Chose*—he saw a "refined and picturesque head. . . . A brilliant talker & raconteur. A Bohemian. An extreme imitator of Dickens—but *à froid*, without Dickens's real exuberance." Daudet, increasingly paralyzed and using a bath chair to visit monuments, was compared so often to the Christ figure as to irritate James. Once he had taken Daudet, visiting London, to meet the great George Meredith, with white hair and a white beard, and quite as paralyzed as Daudet himself. "The dark-eyed meridional and the blue-eyed Briton embraced." (Edel 4, 136)

Gosse tells us of an evening spent with Daudet, whose gift of description was inimitable: "in a moment, we saw before us the masses of golden-yellow and crimson and sea-green fruit in the little white market-place, with the incomparable light of a Provençal harvest morning bathing it all in crystal." (Edel 3, 135) This meeting with such a charming talker renewed James's sense of the high superiority of French talk."

Among his acquaintances in 1889, there was Hippolyte Taine (N, 53 Sunday, May 19, 1889)—"remarkably pleasant," far milder and more genial, said James, than he had been led to believe by his "hard, splendid, intellectual, logical style and manner." (NB53 Sunday, May 19, 1889) He was a charming talker, said James, and had "much more bonhomie, mildness and geniality, than his hard, spelndid, intellectual, logical style and manner had led me to expect." James felt Taine's conversation renewing his sense "of the high superiority of French talk."

Early on James, with his flawless French diction, thanks to his French governesses, was warmly welcomed in Paris. Turgenev, whom James had always wanted to meet, lived at no. 50 rue de Douai. He was tall, with a large frame. The two became friendly by 1879; they corresponded and spoke in French, and Turgenev shared his pessimism gladly. (Edel 2, 204) Turgenev writes him in

George Sand

Paul
Zoukovskye,
1875

French: "La Fortune n'aime
pas les vieillards—meme
en littérature." The Russian
writer was in the beginning
the one to introduce James
to Flaubert and George
Sand. James was enor-
mously fond of him: "I
found him adorable. He
was so simple, so natural,
so modest, so destitute of
personal pretension . . . a
singularly complete human
being." He was under the
thumb of his mistress
Pauline Viardot, so that
when James and his young
friend Paul Zoukovskye
(James's close friend, who
later became such a fer-
vent disciple of Wagner)
wanted to see him, they
would all have lunch at a
café, in order to avoid the
mistress.

James became part of
the circle who gathered
around Flaubert and
Turgenev at Flaubert's
Sunday afternoons on the
Faubourg Rue St. Honoré,
including the whole "*côterie*
of the young realists in
fiction," who included
Edmond de Goncourt,

Portrait of
Gustave
Flaubert,
*Eugène
Giraud, 1856*

Alphonse Daudet and Emile Zola.(Kaplan, 167) Flaubert, receiving on those afternoons from one o'clock until seven, would open the door himself, with his "serious, sober face . . . a powerful, serious, melancholy, deeply corrupted, yet not corrupting, nature." James greatly liked him: "He is an excellent old fellow, simply, naif, & *convaincu*, in his own line, & extremely kind & friendly, not to say affectionate." Flaubert wore a "long colloquial dressing gown with trousers to match." James found this a perfect garb for the writer. But he felt in the works of Flaubert a certain chill, something perhaps "ungenerous"—for in his letters there is only the beauty of words, not of life. (221) Flaubert would read to him from Gautier:

> J'aime à vous voir en vos cadres ovales
> *Portraits jaunis des belles du vieux temps*

James's *Ambassadors* is filled with just such yellowed or yellowing oldtime portraits—which makes the injunction: "Live! Live all you can!" all the more poignant. There are faded pastels in the *Sacred Fount,* an oval frame in the *Ambassadors*; and, in *The Wings*

of the Dove, Milly Theale will become, like the long dead lady in the portrait she stares at, a faded picture, on her way out of the world, like Minny Temple. This time in Paris was a golden one, as if blurred over in memory. despite his many contacts, he was always to wish there had been more time: "how many more strange flowers one *might* have gathered up and preserved."

Minny Temple, at 16, with short hair cropped during an illness,1868

A splendid host to his French friends in London, James was at his easiest introducing them to the British. Among the many French writers with whom James had associated in Paris and who then came over to London on a visit, there was Paul Bourget (113) whom he described as a "rather flabby-looking Frenchman, with a pronounced myopia, an unstable glass in one eye, and a shy manner"; but on the other hand, his literary sense and clever conversation—despite his affected manner and his pronounced anti-Semitism—and his close friendship with Edith Wharton, increasingly a companion for James, made him welcome. James took him to dinner at the Reform Club and was able to introduce him to Edmund Gosse. James would frequently invite his close friend Georges du Maurier to join whatever dinner party he was hosting, usually at the Reform Club, often with other French-speakers in London: the painter Alma-Tadema, Burne-Jones, and Edmund Gosse.

On another occasion, James invited Maupassant, with Gosse and George du Maurier, to dinner, but in the summer, when his club was closed, they took the little steamer down to Greenwich for a seafood supper, on August 12, 1886, an expedition that the guests fondly remembered. Much of the atmosphere of this evening and others may have made its way over to the famous scene in *The Ambassadors* so often likened to an Impressionist painting, when Strether sees Chad and Mme de Vionnet in a boat, and the straw-colored wine and the omelet laid on what we see as a sunstruck luncheon table. James's ultimate tricountry sensitivity infuses his writing as his life.

Edith, Morton, and Henry

Edith Wharton, who had wanted to meet James for a long time, and finally did so, was to become importantly and increasingly, for James, a perfect friend. She came from a distinguished New York family, with whose members James remained in touch. As she says in *A Backward Glance*, they were introduced by Edward Boit and his wife in the late 1880's; she and her husband Teddy next saw him in 1889 or 1890 in Venice—both times she tried to appeal to him by wearing a designer dress and a new hat. On his return trip in 1904 to the United States—sailing into the New York harbor on an August day, before leaving to

see his family in a glorious New England September—he stayed in the house of Wharton's sister-in-law, Mary Cadwalader Jones, except for a week in the 885 Park Avenue town house of Teddy and Edith Wharton (a double brownstone built in the 1880's) and a week in the West Tenth Street house of Lawrence Godkin, son of *The Nation's* editor. This house figures in the story "The Jolly Corner," and Henry wrote to Mrs. Jones: "My New York of those dear East Eleventh Street 'first-floor-back' hours lives again for me as I write . . . it's astonishing, it's

Left: Edith Wharton

Right: Teddy Wharton, 1896

prodigious, how I find my spirit gratefully haunting them always—or rather how insidiously turning the tables they, the mystic locality itself, haunt and revisit my own departed identity." (Bell, 15)

Edith Newbold Jones was in some sense a counterpart of the James who had chosen to live somewhere else than Boston. "Too shy to perform in the Boston social milieu, she carried with her a suppressed but restless sense of alienation and desperation." (Kaplan, 481) Part of Edith's intense energy, in her writing and her living, came precisely from her uneasiness in society—thus the rushing about. James described her frenetic lifestyle as not altogether positive for other people, including himself: her "general eagle-power pounces and eagle-flight of her deranging and desolating, ravaging, burning and destroying energy . . . the Angel of Devastation was the mildest name we knew her by." (Benstock, 197) And yet, of course, it was that energy that she put also in her friendship, valuable to him until the end of his life.

Edith Wharton wrote novel after novel, was highly respected and well paid—James was often to tease her about that, about the difference between her grand style of living from her royalties and his humble way of being, his royalties sufficient only to purchase a wheelbarrow in which to receive his visitors' suitcases. The amusing image is, as often the case in James, true enough. The devoted and sociable Jonathan Sturges, a friend of Whistler, and translator of some of Maupassant's stories, early crippled by polio, who spent long periods at Lamb House, found which bags belonged to whom and trundled them up the road to Lamb House.

In 1906, James spent three rainy days rushing about France in the Panhard of the Whartons, those "rich, rushing, ravening Whartons." (Kaplan, 505) For him, the hotels they frequented were far too expensive, and the Panhard automobile seemed a "chariot of fire" as they sped about from George Sand's Nohant to Burgundy to Provence and to Lourdes, Pau, and the Pyrenees. It makes a wonderful picture, the three of them wearing their goggles in the car, hurtling along on its thin, airless tires. Needless to say, the Whartons' servants were sent before, everywhere, to make ready. Not James's kind of life at all.

Facing page:
Morton
Fullerton

Enter the dapper charmer Morton Fullerton, whom James met in 1890, who had a post in the London *Times* bureau in Paris, where he spent the next 25 years, switching to *Le Figaro*, where he would write in French about American culture and affairs. Well-dressed, with a perfectly groomed mustache and a slim figure, Fullerton was the object of much affection, female and male. Fullerton had had many homosexual affairs with those in the circle of Oscar Wilde, notably in the 1880's in London with the sculptor Ronald Sutherland, Lord Gower, who brought him together with James. Fullerton, always in some emotional scrape, had had a liaison with the Ranee of Sarawak, Margaret Brooke (the estranged wife of the Rajah, James Brooke), to whom James had presented him, had had a longstanding affair with the Parisian Henrietta Mirecourt in 1903, had married Victoria Camille Chabert, one year later, and was involved with a young cousin teaching at Bryn Mawr, Katherine Fullerton—who had arranged his lecture on Henry James, at Bryn Mawr in 1907, and who believed he was about to marry her.

Fullerton was a highly attractive man—his magnetism enhanced for Henry James, no doubt, by his multiple other interests. Morton spent a November night in the fall of 1907 at Lamb House. Henry loved it, and Morton: "My difficulty is that I love you too fantastically much. . . . You touch and penetrate me to the quick, and I can only stretch out my hand to draw you closer." (Kaplan, 511). His desire for more of Morton, undying over the years, was palpable, as in this letter of September 26, 1900: "My life is arranged—if arranged it can be called—on the lines of constantly missing you . . . I want in fact more of you. You are dazzling . . . you are beautiful; you are more than tactful, you are tenderly, magically *tactile*. But you're not kind." (Edel, *Letters*, 180) James loved to hint, every suggestion feeling erotic to the extreme. In other letters to Fullerton, he almost mentions "incidents" that he could tell him only were he right there. In this superflirtatious or supersuggestive writing, this super-purple prose, we recognize James, and what in anyone else would be hard to stomach is stomachable. How could we even envisage that James the writer would be writing a simple love letter like anyone else?

The Mount

It had been Henry James's letter of introduction for Fullerton to Edith Wharton which had brought Fullerton to Lenox in the fall of 1907. Above all, perhaps, as a novelist and a person, James was a good gossip, loved the art of gossiping, and made a grand confidant. Thus, his deep involvement with the Morton Fullerton–Edith Wharton affair, which came to a glorious threeway meeting of June 1909, pictured in James's notebook. James enjoyed this pattern of involvement, as he had with Margaret Brooke and Fullerton—a vicarious pleasure.

Edith Wharton, like many others, fell deeply in love with Fullerton on his visit to the Mount in October of 1907. Upon his leaving, on October 22, she began her "Love Diary," called "L'Âme close," and in February of 1908, after visiting a village close to Paris wrote a poem with the same title, centered around an image of her sentimental feeling—her seemingly unlit heart:

Yet one stray passer, at the shut of day,
Sees a light trembling in a casement high,
Even so, my soul would set a light for you,
A light invisible to all beside. (Benstock, 178)

But of course, Morton had other interests. By October, 1908, Edith had confided to Henry everything about the affair with Morton, with whom she was desperately involved, pointing out that her marriage to the very rich and boring Teddy Wharton had become unbearable. Then in that November Edith and her close friend, the always bachelor lawyer Walter Van Rensselaer Berry, visited James at Lamb House, where the Master loved having visitors to relieve the somewhat monotonous atmosphere of the small village of Rye. The next June, in 1909, Henry shared a champagne dinner with the lovers in the Charing Cross Hotel—quite visibly not at all the kind of hotel to which Edith was accustomed, which would rather be Claridge's near Berkeley Square, or then the Berkeley, in Piccadilly. (Henry James had had a taste of Edith's normal hotels on the rapid drive about France with the Whartons so long ago.) Now, though, this hotel at a busy London crossroads was exactly the kind of place needed for her affair, and for James's vicarious involvement in it. Edith and Morton had Suite 92 in the hotel, and Henry, greatly appreciative of the situation—so close to the real thing, but not having to be involved in it—returned to the Reform Club for the night. Edith's poem "Terminus" reflects upon that heated occasion, when the erotic encounter was echoed by the "shaking and shrieking of trains, the night-long shudder of traffic." A few months later, her poem "The Room" makes the location the symbolic sentimental container of the lovemaking:

> *O, all my world in the world,*
> *Heart in my breast, O room!*

The note in which she folded the poem, which she wanted Fullerton to return, declared her joy: "Je suis si heureuse—it breaks over me like a great sweet tide." (Benstock, 215-217)

In the morning after the Charing Cross event, Henry saw Morton off to America, and that afternoon, he went out with Edith to Queen's Acre, known familiarly as "Qu'Acre," Howard Sturgis's hospitable home near Windsor, and visited with Howard and "the Babe," his nephew and companion William Haynes-Smith. Here all was warmth, as Howard would

Edith Wharton with two dogs, c. 1884

Henry James, Howard Henry Sturgis, and the Boits,
Vallombrosa, 1907

sit in the center of whatever group he had assembled about him, and
continue his knitting. It was a chosen atmosphere. Percy Lubbock,
often of the company, quotes James, for the intersocial nourishment
on which friendship and the delights of gossip flourished: "Our dear
Howard is like a cake, a richly sugared cake—always on the table. We
sit round him in a circle and help ourselves." (Kaplan, 435)

Five weeks later, together at Lamb House, Edith and Morton returned, for dinner and to spend the night, and the next day, they all lunched at Eastbourne and visited Chichester, full of plans to free the poor and much put-upon Morton from the wily clutches of the terrible and Parisian Henrietta Mirecourt, his former mistress, who had stolen some letters from Morton and was blackmailing him. Nothing could more appeal to the novelists Edith and Henry, who figured out a plot, a rescue, in full libertarian righteousness. The rescue worked—Edith transferred money to James, and he to Macmillan, for Fullerton as an advance on a book which he never wrote, with which he paid the Mirecourt off, ignorant of the sum's source.

Morton and Edith were not to remain together for always—of course not, says the reader. James put it perfectly in a letter to Edith of May 24, 1914: "the non-eventuation of him." (Edel 5, 532) And in fact, Edith and Teddy were not divorced until April 1913, while the affair with Fullerton was over by 1910. In Edith's life, if not her bed, Walter Berry ("the love of all my life") took Morton's place, and all three remained friends, occasionally dining together. But the pain of Morton's involvement with so many others was not to be forgotten by Henry James. It was all a "*personal* waste, that of something—ah, so tender!—in *me* that was only quite yearningly ready for you, and something all possible, and all deeply and admirably appealing in yourself, of which I never got the benefit." (Kaplan, 511.) Perhaps not, but something of the delicious desire remaining desire—as in the later surrealists' longing for recreation of sexual and emotional energy—remains as an intense source of the jottings in the notebook and in the novels.

Minny Temple, 1869

Loves, Losses, and Involvements

Looking back, much of James's life might be seen to be about loss as much as about affection. These mingled strangely, and seem to have left no residue of bitterness at the various losses or of caution about future involvements. His folding in on himself was in no way a contradiction to his highly active social life, applying rather to his interior being. The famous burning of his papers—which he carried out once in 1909, and then again later, from Lamb House, in order not to leave so many strands for future biographers—gives anyone speculating about his life its own interesting mystery on which to muse, and a certain freedom to do so. We have just what is left: that is already a lot.

One of the most important losses for Henry, although far less obvious a loss than the death of his younger sister Alice, was his cousin Minny Temple's death at an early age. She had been luminous for him, with the "moral spontaneity" and "intellectual grace" he also found in Clover Hooper Adams. Writing this to William, he could not realize that she had just died on the day he wrote, March 8, 1870. It was all the more terrible, because she had just expressed the desire to go over to Rome with Henry. Vivid and intense, "flame-like and beloved," Minny had been, in James's youth, the person most alive in his mind, most radiant: (Nozick, 221) Minny "seemed such a breathing immortal reality that the mere statement of her death conveys little meaning . . ." Milly Theale in the *Wings of the Dove* has much of Minny Temple, of that "wonderful ethereal brightness of presence which was so peculiarly her own."

But always, haunting the entire family, was Alice. Alice always something of an enigma, enthusiastic and sickly. "Victimization as career," says one of James's biographers (Kaplan, 87). Always her nerves. Alice was jealous, or at least envious of Minny, taking her as a sort of rival. "She is not nearly so interesting as she used to be," said Alice one day of her cousin. (Kaplan, 76) In May of 1872, Henry and his Aunt Kate and Alice had all gone over to Europe, and he had booked their return voyage in October on the same ship, the *Algeria,* which had brought them over, from England to Switzerland, where they were joined by friends of the James family, Francis Boott and his daughter Lizzie, who lived back and forth between Boston and Bellosguardo near Florence. In the Swiss mountains, Alice often fell ill. She was better in cities than in mountain resorts, it turned out. To Italy and Austria—unbeloved by Henry: "What colossal tastelessness," he

Alice James, June 1870

Elizabeth Boott

said at Innsbruck, of a typical inn. (Edel 2, 67) They left, and Henry stayed.

When later, with her companion Katherine Loring, she traveled to Europe, Henry accompanied them around, and when she was settled in London in 1891, in South Kensington, he called upon her every day. To her he was as attentive as to the characters in his novels. At the end of her life there developed a sense that death was a bit long in coming: she kept working at it, as she repeatedly said. Her final telegram to her family, already quoted, expresses her relief: "Tenderest love to all. Farewell. Am going soon. Alice."

When, on March 5, 1892, Alice died, a few hours after dictating that cable, the cremation was arranged, and the ashes taken to be placed alongside the graves of her parents. Henry was overcome with grief and when he eventually made his way to her grave in

Alice James in Kensington, June 1891

Cambridge, alongside others in the family, he felt he had come back to America and saw "why I had come: the recognition, stillness, the passion of the divine relief of tears." (Kaplan, 485)

Constance Fenimore Woolson

The most haunting loss of all—apart from that of Henry's beloved and difficult brother William, his protector and intimate—was that of Constance Fenimore Woolson, a descendant of James Fenimore Cooper, whom Henry called Fenimore. Deaf in one ear, no longer young, never lovely in appearance, Constance was an accomplished novelist and someone always in tune with James. Solitary, she had been accustomed to taking lonely walks by herself at the end of hot days on the edge of rice fields, skirting swamplands and observing the death-in-life of the South, talking to Negroes, as she made notes on their dialect for her book "Roman the Keeper: Southern Sketches." (Kaplan, 222)

James had spent a great deal of time with her in Florence, in the spring of 1880, when he was at the Hôtel de l'Arno, and she at Madame Barbensi's pension on the Lung'Arno, in London, and at Bellosguardo, a hill overlooking Florence. There she was a great friend of the Bootts, to whom James had written when Constance left England, asking them to watch over her a bit, at Villa Brichieri-Colombi that she had leased at Bellosguardo, and where James spent some time. That they did from their Villa Castellani, which had been designed in the fifteenth century by a follower of Michelangelo, and which served as a center for Anglo-American painters, friends of the family.

Right: Villa Brichieri-Colombi, Bellosgardo

Below: Villa Castellani, Bellosgardo

Pink Roses in a Vase *by Elizabeth Boott Duveneck, 1883*

Constance grew particularly close to Lizzie, the Boott daughter who was portrayed as Pansy in *Portrait of a Lady*, set in the Villa Castellani. Lizzie was also a great friend of Alice James (to whom she dedicated her *Pink Roses in a Vase* of 1883). Like William James, she had studied with William Morris Hunt, and then with Thomas Couture near Paris. She was to study with and eventually marry an Ohioan painter, two years her junior, the "uncouth but vigorous" Frank Duveneck (Kaplan, 22), whose work she admired. She wrote to a friend in 1879, when she was studying with him in Munich, how "the paint seems to squirm round at his bidding in the most extraordinary manner and model itself . . . He is a child of nature but a natural gentleman. He seems to have led the queerest, most vagrant sort of life . . . He is the frankest, kindest-hearted of mortals." (Duveneck, 7-9) Duveneck

Frank Duveneck, Venice, 1874

taught after that in Florence—the period of his Italian style—where Lizzie continued as his student, and where he was surrounded by his male students, his "boys." His work varied from his dark Munich style through the Italian period to the far brighter Paris paintings. In 1880, he was in Venice with his "boys" and part of Whistler's circle. He was, everywhere he went, an adored teacher and friend. James, hearing of their marriage in March of 1886 in Paris, wrote to a friend that Duveneck was "illiterate, ignorant, and not a gentleman. His talent is great, though without delicacy. But I fear his indolence is greater still. Lizzie, however, will urge him forward and be an immense help to him. For him it is all gain; for her it is very brave." (Kentucky Post) Yet James still greatly admired Duveneck's painting, writing to Charles Eliot Norton, teaching art history at Harvard, that he was "the most highly developed phenomenon in the way of a painter that the U.S.A. [had] given birth to." (Duveneck, 13). Lizzie had made the proviso, after breaking off their engagement the first time, five years before, not being able to bear to leave her father, that this time she not be separated from him. Francis Boott was a composer who had

Harmony in Blue and Silver: Trouville, *by James Abbott McNeill Whistler*

The Libyan Sibyl,
William Wetmore Story,
1868

set "Aftermath" of Henry Wadsworth Longfellow and a poem
of James Russell Lowell to music in Boston, and whose chamber
music was now played at the Palazzo Barberini in Rome, home
of the Boston family of William Wetmore Story, whose biography
James was to write. Shortly after the wedding of the Duvenecks—
when they had returned to Florence—they read together Ruskin's
autobiography, *Praeterita,* which must have been all the more
interesting to Duveneck, since he had spent so much time in
Ruskin's Venice. A child, Charlie, was born before Christmas that
year, and then tragedy struck. Lizzie died of pneumonia in Paris at
42 in March, shortly after Frank's famous portrait of her was

painted. Her body was returned to "Florence, her favorite home . . . there to rest in that beautiful country of flowers," and Frank designed a Tomb Effigy in 1894 for the Campo Santo degli Allori, a marble copy of which he gave to the Museum of Fine Arts in Boston, and a bronze one to the Metropolitan Museum in New York. A palm covers her body, and her long braids surround her head. Henry James described the resting place: "towards the end of April, she was committed to the Florentine earth, in a grave in the Allori Cemetery, beyond the Roman gate, beneath a row of tall cypresses. Great masses of flowers were heaped upon it, and her Florentine friends gathered in large numbers to say farewell." (Kentucky Post)

And then one day, as Leon Edel describes it, "elderly plain deaf devoted Constance Fenimore" left her villa, where she and James had spent so many agreeable moments under the same roof, put it on the market, and moved to London in the fall, and then to 4 Promenade Terrace, Cheltenham. Finally, she departed for Venice, where James had thought, he said, of renting a small apartment. There seems to have been a great deal of discussion about it among Constance and his friends, and he must have felt irritated. Not a good idea, for someone as elusive as the great writer. He might not have wanted the public recognition of them together, although he had recommended her to his friends, who did invite her often. Not enough, though, not enough, if anything would have been enough, without Henry's arrival.

He did not go. Perhaps Constance had hoped for more than she was ever to have had; perhaps she had not understood Henry James. Or then, perhaps she had, with the mind of a novelist—which of course does not necessarily jibe with the heart. Henry writes of himself, "I am too good a bachelor to spoil. That sounds conceited—but one may be conceited, in self-defense, about a position with which the rest of the world associates a certain idea of the ridiculous." (Nozick, 379)

When she was about to leave England, she had written, and we might take these words as her epitaph: "I am giving up being near my kind friend Mr. James." For then Constance, deaf and aging, feeling deserted no doubt, threw herself out a second-floor window on to the pavement. Her death was always to haunt him, understandably, in Venice and elsewhere.

James was so traumatized by the news that he did not go to the funeral. Subsequently, Fenimore's sister Clara Benedict, having come over from America to arrange the funeral and dispose of the remains, enlisted James's help in the latter task. He, of course, had wanted to retrieve his letters to her. Bizarrely, upon his arrival in Venice, a few days after the funeral, he took in the Casa Biondetti, the very same rooms that had been Feminore's until she moved to Casa Semitecolo, and even slept in her bed. The depiction of this entire event in *The Master* is more than masterful. Colm Toíbín describes to perfection the odd scene of his going over her papers evening by evening, disposing of certain ones, questioning the oarsman of her gondola about her last days and her death. Finally, in the world of the novel as in the world of fact, he piled her black dresses into the gondola, had himself rowed out to the lagoon, and threw them in the water, where they rose horribly all around: "Some of the dresses had floated to the surface again like black balloons, evidence of the strange sea burial they had just enacted, their arms and bellies bloated with water;" he was surrounded by them. (Toíbín, 254)

Henry's Fenimore was buried in the Protestant cemetery in Rome, under a shelter of cypress, not far from graves of Shelley and Trelawny, near Keats and Severn. Rome, after all, where Daisy Miller had been interred after dying of Roman fever. Nothing could be more Jamesian than Fenimore's life and

Fanny Kemble

Fenimore's end. (Edel 3, 361)

Some of the remains appear to be stranger than strange. In her library was a book by James, *Essays in London*. In it, his essay on Fanny Kemble bears a note by Fenimore about the following incident. Fanny Kemble, she wrote, had said to her on an evening at the theatre in which James had introduced them to each other, the following: "I am sorry Mr. James has introduced you to me. I shall be obliged to tell you now, that I shall not speak to you, or look at or be conscious of your existence even, during the entire evening." (Edel 3, 368) Stranger still: Constance Fenimore Woolson's name had been erased in the book, and Henry James was written over it. Also, the inscription "Constance Fenimore Woolson from Henry James", also in pencil, was erased, but the name Henry James remains legible. The suggestion of the way it was in real life might well haunt the reader—literary remains indeed.

In her notebook are several entries more suggestive still of the way it was:

> To imagine a person (woman) always misunderstood; considered shy, sullen, cold, etc. simply because she has never had about her people who really like her.

> A love story. It tells how she loved him. He did not think of her at all; in fact he never noticed her.

And this one, the probable source for "The Beast in the Jungle."

> To imagine a man spending his life looking for and waiting for his "splendid moment." . . . But the moment never comes. When he is old and infirm it comes to a neighbour who has never thought of it or cared for it. (Edel 3, 370)

In one of Constance's stories, a woman writer takes a manuscript to a successful writer, who, taking apart her text and its "figure in the carpet," unravels it. If this figure in this carpet was to haunt him always, leading to his own figured carpet, it is no less the case that all these three women, the sister, the early friend, and the dramatically involved Fenimore, really loved Henry James.

But, since Parisian days, says Fred Kaplan, James had been conscious of his own homoeroticism, repressed as it was. (Kaplan, 300) In 1877, he met John Addington Symonds, whose treatise on homosexuality, *A Problem of Modern Ethics*, of 1891, had to be published privately. Gosse, sharing Symonds's tendencies, had showed Henry James some of Symonds's papers also, being of like persuasion, and James's own stories such as "The Pupil," and "The Author of Beltraffio" are full of suggestive passages, along these lines. James followed with great interest Oscar Wilde's trial in 1895, much as he disliked "the unspeakable one's" flamboyancy.

In the mid 1890's, James fell in love many times. Wonderfully, these affections included the small and sweet-faced Jonathan Sturges, slightly crippled, always around, always helpful: "He is only a little boy—blighted brilliant intelligence, a little frustrated universal curiosity." (Kaplan, 401) And there were others. Among the persons he loved were three who stand out, themselves vivid: the dapper and deceptive Morton Fullerton, deserving of his own chapter with Edith Wharton and our Henry; Jocelyn Persse; and Hendrik Anderson.

These years were clearly ones of awakening. Incident after incident: in 1899, James makes a visit with Mrs. Humphrey Ward to Ariccia, to see home of Egeia, known as "the sacred fount," so the source itself of that bizarre and high camp eponymous novel. Here in Ariccia James sees a young boy named Aristodemo, and writes later: "for me, the Nemi lake, and the walk down and up (the latter perhaps most), and the strawberries and Aristodemo were the cream" (TR 297-8.) In the novel's central scene, that of the art gallery, a concealed homosexual relation gives the scene away, perhaps, and about this "picture, of all pictures, that most needs an interpreter. *Don't* we want . . . to know what it means?"

> *The figure represented is a young man in black—a quaint, tight black dress, fashioned in years long past; with a pale, lean, livid face and a stare, from eyes without eyebrows, like that of some whitened old-world clown. In his hand he holds an object that strikes the spectator at first simply as some obscure, some ambiguous work of art, but that on a second view becomes a representation of a human face, modelled and coloured, in wax, in enameled metal, in some substance not human. The object thus appears a complete mask, such as might have been fantastically fitted and worn.* (Sacred Fount, 50-51)

How to know which is life, the mask, "blooming and beautiful," "charmingly pretty," or the man's own face; as in a ghost story, the former is more probable. Inversion, of life and death, and genders: the mask is likely that of a woman.

Several of James's stories and novels center about a cross-dressing and cross-naming situation, my favorite being "The Death of the Lion," (T179), in which "Guy Walsingham," a pretty girl writer suggests a "larger latitude" of thinking. James's friend Rhoda Broughton's *Dear Faustina*, was, according to Richard Ellman, the "first lesbian novel in English." In 1895, James was asked to participate in a petition to free Oscar Wilde, drawn up by Stuart Merrill, an American symbolist poet. But James said it would do no good, and regretted that Wilde seemed to have no resistance of his own.

Oscar Wilde, by Henri de Toulouse-Lautrec, 1895

Bust of Henry James by Hendrik Anderson

In any case, at some point James the public writer and James the private person converged. The most celebrated of James's suggestive relations was with the Danish sculptor Hendrik Andersen, creator of large and ambitious works of art, and for whom James felt much. Andersen had visited him in the late summer of 1899, and the relation, increasingly explicit, lasted, but with few meetings between the parties. Henry loved Hendrik. "He bestowed on Andersen his own taste, his own high standards, his own feeling for beauty." (Edel 4, 309) James kept by him the small head of Bevilaqua—which he much preferred to the very large and ambitious statues Andersen was fond of creating. Over and over in his letters, he longs for Andersen: in 1904, "your poor helpless far-off but all devoted H.J.;" as in 1905 and 1906: "we don't meet"; until 1911, when the sixty-eight year old James is still writing in the same vein to the thirty-nine year old Hendrik: "I want to see you—and I so hold out my arms to you." (Edel 4, 314)

In this same year, James saw Jocelyn Persse of Galway, the nephew of Lady Gregory, whom we associate with the poet Yeats. Persse was a handsome well-connected Irishman with blond hair whom he had met in 1903. James, writing of Persse, perhaps happily not much of an intellectual, describes "his constituted *aura* of fine gold and rose-colour." (Edel 5, 183) Persse was totally at ease in his social whirl, and James loves exactly that: "I envy you the magnificent ease with which you circulate & revolve . . . spinning round like a brightly-painted top that emits, as it goes, only the most musical hum; . . . the mysterious genial power that guides & sustains you through the multitude of your contacts & the mazes of your dance." (Kaplan, 475)

The difference between them is in no way bothersome to Henry James: no anguish attaches to it, rather something quite positive. "I quite rejoice in the bright brave vision of you . . . Even while I crouch in my corner . . . through you, the vibration of adventure and the side-wind of the unfolding panorama." (Edel 5, 185) And again, "I want to hold on to *you*." When Persse had been to Greece, James wanted to experience through the younger man everything, treasuring the "dear, dear Jocelyn, for all your sensations & notations." Feeling a "silver cord" between the two of them, he declared himself "addicted to the intimate visions and thoughts of you." Later, in November of 1909 at Ockham, they spent two miraculous days together. James writes of them "Nov. 27th-29th in those fantastic contiguous apartments. . . . I reach out to you with a sort of tender frenzy." (Kaplan, 513-15) Looking back, he remembers three wonderful days spent together, rather like the long and perfect weekend spent with Hendrik Andersen.

These brief times with Andersen, with Persse were perhaps just what James most treasured. Nothing long and boringly drawn out, but a continuous reawakening of desire—James was a true modern. Persse was later to declare, "Why he liked me so much I cannot say . . . [he was] the dearest human being I have ever known." (Edel 5, 188)

James all his life kept, it seems, the memory of those beloved younger men. In his later years, James saw more of the far younger writer Hugh Walpole, whom he had met in 1909, and who was the last of James's young men. For the record, and for history, Walpole made the pronouncement that he had once propositioned James, who said "I cannot, I can't." (Kaplan, 559)

Perhaps he could not, then or before—how are we to know? —but what he left as memories of the desire he could feel quite suffices for us.

Art and Letters

Henry James, consummate writer, spent his life, we can scarcely fail to observe, in an intense appreciation of his own art and that of others. The struggle between "life" and "art" was at once constant and vivifying. Paradoxically, one of his most valuable assets was his deeply-sensed apartness: (Nozick, 391) "The port from which I set out was, I think, that of the essential loneliness of my life—and it seems also . . . to which my course again finally directs itself! That loneliness. . . what is it still but the deepest thing about one?" The other side of this—and all the more valuable for that reason, so that the condition and the antidote were equally vivid—was the feeling of the community of creating individuals: that which permitted him to occasionally use the collective first-person plural pronoun. One of the most famous passages from the part of his autobiography called "The Middle Years" speaks to this: (Kaplan, 372) "I want to do what they call live. . . . We work in the dark—we do what we can—we give what we have. Our doubt is our passion and our passion is our task."

His "eye" was always good, in his memory and in his ongoing work. He remembered, as a child on a trip to Paris, his first visit to the Louvre. Its paintings "arched over us in the wonder of their endless golden riot and relief, figured and flourished in perpetual revolution, breaking into great high-hung circles and symmetries of squandered picture, opening into deep outward embrasures that threw off the rest of monumental Paris somehow as a told story, a sort of wrought effect or bold ambiguity for a vista, and yet held it there, at every point, as a vast bright gage, even at moments a felt adventure, of experience." (Auto, 195-6) In particular, he was struck by the Galerie d'Apollon—designed by Louis Le

Henry James,
c. 1906

Vau, under Louis XIV, and just restored in 2004 in all its ceremonial splendor, a model for the Hall of Mirrors at Versailles, with its paintings by Le Brun and Delacroix, and its 50-foot ceilings and gilded woodwork: "the wondrous Galerie d'Apollon, drawn out for me as a long but assured initiation and seeming to form with its supreme coved ceiling and inordinately shining parquet a prestigious tube or tunnel through which I inhaled little by little, that is again and again, a general sense of *glory*." (Auto, 196) Its "deep embrasures and the so polished floor" remained in his memory. That memory was visual and precise, a good thing for a novelist, and for someone who was to circulate so widely in the artistic worlds of Paris and London. Delacroix was an early enthusiasm of the James brothers and remained one: "we were to go on seeing him, and to the end, in firm possession of his crown, and to take even, I think, a harmless pleasure in our sense of having from so far back been sure of it . . . ." He was for them "ineffable, inscrutable, and incalculable." (Auto, 195)

Eugène Delacroix, Self-Portrait

Many of his friends in the literary and artistic world were eccentric—appealing to his own psychology with its tendency toward habitual behavior. Occasionally, as was the case with the American painter James Abbott McNeill Whistler, as much of an eccentric as a genius, James was to grow increasingly admiring of the person and the work. More and more, he began to appreciate Whistler's suggestive and understated painting—as well as the not understated painter and his famous Sunday breakfasts in his garden house at 110 rue du Bac in Paris or at his London home. In London, James went in mid-April to one of these Whistler's "somewhat classical" Sunday breakfasts at his "queer-little house in Chelsea, on the river . . . He is a queer little Londonized Southerner. . . ." Whistler cooks abominably, says James. But his breakfasts are easy and pleasant, and he has "tomatoes and buckwheat cakes." Moreover James increasingly came to understand the painting and the wit of the life. (Kaplan, 193) And at one of Whistler's Paris breakfasts in the little interior garden at 110 rue du Bac, when James was visiting from London, he met the handsome and on-the-way-to-famous painter John Singer Sargent, twelve years his junior, first a pupil and then a rival of the celebrated Carolus-Duran. (Edel 3, 111)

Born in Italy, and never even visiting the United States until he was an adult, Sargent nevertheless considered himself an American.

Having grown up in a family as peripatetic as that of James, he spoke, like James, a flawless and unaccented French. Together the three of them make a fascinating triptych, Whistler (born in Russia), Sargent, and James, spending their lives in Paris and London, these American expatriates sooner or later or from always, surrounded by the intelligentsia of old Europe, and endowed with a special kind of resplendently creative American energy. James was, it seems, instantly smitten by Sargent. Before meeting the painter, he had praised Sargent's *Fumée d'Ambre Gris* of 1880 as "exquisite" and "radiant," and then continued to extol his work, which he tirelessly promoted, saying that Sargent saw "each work that he provides in a light of its own," unlike most other portrait-painters. (Davis, 226) He

Caricature of John Singer Sargent *by* Max Beerbohm, *1910*

Study of Mme. Gautreau, *John Singer Sargent*, 1904

was less enthusiastic about Sargent's portrait of Amélie Gautreau, *Madame X*, which provoked such a scandal, with her white-powdered face, her rouge-tipped ears, and one bejeweled strap falling down her shoulder as if threatening to expose her under her tight black dress with its tiny waist. James's story "The Pupil" was inspired by Sargent's early story, quite like his own, with their nomadic childhoods and the lack of psychological security conferred by more stable and anchored upbringings. In any case, the somewhat mysterious lives of both men makes any speculation tempting, and James seemed to play the same role in his attraction to Sargent (as in that to Paul Joukowsky, Anderssen, and Persse) as that of Sargent in his infatuation with the seductive doctor Samuel Pozzi, the socialite Amélie Gautreau, the orientalist Judith Gautier, and the young artist Albert de Belleroche.

James acted as genial host on Sargent's visits to London, beginning in 1884, introducing the painter to all the artists he longed to meet. James's hosts in Venice at the Palazzo Barbaro, the Ralph Curtises, were Sargent's cousins, and the immensely wealthy collector Isabella Stewart Gardner, whom Sargent was to paint with her extraordinary necklace of pearls circling her waist, was James's host in that Palazzo when she rented it from the Curtises. (The museum that bears her name in Boston's Fenway Court is modeled on the

78   *Henry James*

fifteenth-century Palazzo Barbaro on the Grand Canal, which greatly profited from her money and her taste.) The tales of her deliciously unBostonian behaviour are rampant, and all the more delightful, not only about the Musicales in her "Tapestry Room," beyond criticism as was the art she collected, but of her "perennially attracting rumors of sensual excess: she lined a room with black velvet or posed nude for a group of gentlemen artists. She repented a transgression by scrubbing the steps of the Episcopal church of the Advent on Good Friday," says Honor Moore in her preface to the poems of Amy Lowell, the imagist poet (whose imitators and followers Ezra Pound mocked as "Amygists"). Mrs. Jack, as she was called, entertained in her home not just James but "her sometime lover, the novelist Francis Marion Crawford," Moore continues, remarking that her very unconventionality was an inspiration to Lowell. (Lowell, xxv) Unconventional she was, taking her pet leopard shopping and elsewhere. Having been raised as a Protestant, she became, in her own terms, more Catholic than the Pope. Choosing the then unfashionable Anglican Church of the Advent—whose steps she did indeed scrub with brush and bucket every Ash Wednesday, and to which she gave a lofty reredos, three to four stories high—she left instructions that at her funeral, as with royalty, the pallbearers were to carry her coffin on their shoulders, not at waist level as is the usual custom. She gave land to the monks of the Society of St. John the Evangelist across the river in Cambridge, and on her birthday, those monks or clergy from the Advent celebrate mass in her private chapel in the museum.

But despite all that, fashion being the fickle thing it is, she was "too amiable to become *really* fashionable," James wrote to Mrs. Curtis, "She tries too hard and listens too sympathetically . . ." (ED2, 381). In short, a lady of admirable character. It was, unsurprisingly enough, James who had introduced Mrs. Jack to Sargent's studio in October of 1886.

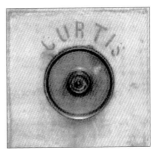

Curtis doorbell, Venice

James and Sargent would meet often in Broadway, a small village in the Cotswolds, at the welcoming home of Frank and Lily Millet, where there gathered other artists and also James's great friend Edmund Gosse, with his wife and sister-in-law, married to that painter of exotica, Lawrence Alma-Tadema. There Sargent, another Wagnerian devotee like James's friend Paul Zoukovsky, would sing from one or another Wagnerian opera.

In Paris, Sargent was in frequent company with and correspondence with the outlandish Comte de Montesquiou-Fezensac, the leading model for Proust's Baron de Charlus, and for the super-decadent character des Esseintes in Joris-Karl Huysman's *A Rebours* (*Against the Grain*). Des Esseintes was fond of everything artificial, inserting jewels in his tortoise's shell, liking white roses that would resemble cotton, and taking trips to London in a ship's stateroom outfitted like an English club, from which he never issued forth.

Once Whistler came to London with Montesquiou, who used to describe himself physically as a greyhound in a great-

Statue of Wagner, Venice

Robert, Comte de Montesquiou-Fezensac, James Abbot McNeill Whistler

coat, and mentally as the "sovereign of transitory things," and whom James found both "curious" and "slight." (Edel 3, 150) James invited the two visitors to dinner, the dandyish Whistler with his white forelock and the "Fatal Count," with the Prince de Polignac. At this occasion, continuing the bizarreries of the situation, Whistler asked James to write to George H. Boughton, who could show the Fatal Count the place where Whistler had painted his more than celebrated *Peacock Room*, commissioned by Frederick Leland—and the subject of much argument between the patron and the painter, over the outlandish expense. Oddest of all, James thought, was the fact that he, writing the letter, would not be there at the showing, but, as he pointed out, "on the whole nothing that relates to Whistler is any queerer than anything else." This was perhaps part of his attraction for James.

Among other eccentrics, James particularly loathed Oscar Wilde, whose relation to Whistler was anything but calm. Whistler's stance toward Wilde can be summed up best by the perhaps apocryphal story of Oscar saying to Whistler about some Whistlerian *bon mot* that he wished he had said it, and Whistler replying: "You will, Oscar, you will." When Whistler was out of town and unable to attend one of his beloved poet friend Stéphane Mallarmé's Tuesday receptions, he sent a wire to the poet: "O. is coming. Lock up the silver." James agreed with Whistler about many things, and in particular about Wilde. He found the play *Lady Windermere's Fan* to be "of a candid and primitive simplicity, with a perfect reminiscent air about it." (Edel 4, 44) There was, admittedly,

car Wilde,
x Beerbohm,
2

he said, much drollery, many epigrams and *bons mots*. But he found it just as strained as always ("equally strained Oscar") and the situation so boring and predictable as any that "one has seen from the cradle." (Edel 4, 45) In Paris, Henry wrote, "the unspeakable one made his speech to the audience, with a metallic blue carnation in his buttonhole and a cigarette in his fingers . . ." Between the Fatal Count, the quite improbable Whistler, and the Unspeakable One, James's world was peopled with unusual characters, to say the least.

Of course, the bitterness of its having been an enthusiastic audience reception of Wilde's play that James attended just before the disastrous reception of his own, the illfated *Guy Domville*, was all the greater for the comparison of himself and the Unspeakable One. When George Alexander came out on stage after the uproar and apologized, someone in the gallery called out, "'Taint your fault, guv'nor, it's a rotten play!" (Edel 4, 80) After the ghastly event, which marked James's utter disappointment with the theatre, he reflected, (Edel 4, 63) "I may have been meant for the Drama—God knows! but I certainly wasn't meant for the Theatre." However, he recovered: "Large and full and high the future still opens. It is now indeed that I may do the work of my life. And I will." And that he did.

The actors he himself enjoyed included Sarah Bernhardt, whom he saw in *L'Aiglon* and *La Princesse Lointaine*, and Coquelin in *Cyrano de Bergerac,* where the actor magnificently swaggered, both sentimental and sublime. In London he saw Eleanora Duse, whose "exquisite delicacy and truth and naturalness" he greatly admired, with her "pathos, a finish and absence of the tricks of the trade that are strangely touching and fascinating. No beauty— no wigs, no clothes, scarcely any paint—but a delicate refinement and originality. The total is rare." (Edel 4, 47) In his discussion of the two actresses, Edel compares the temperament of Bernhardt with Oscar Wilde, and that of the Duse, with James's own. H. G. Wells, at that point a critic for the *Pall Mall Gazette*—called Henry James "a sensitive man lost in an immensely abundant brain." (Edel 4, 69) (Never an enthusiast of James, he wrote a pitiless

Sarah Bernhardt as Phèdre

spoof of his writing in his 1915 *Boon*.) In a sense, the dichotomy between "drama" and "theatre" was the same as that between writing for serious publication and for lighter ones. While James wanted to write serious pieces, the *Tribune* wanted gossip. His pieces on Paris, on Chartres, on the "cool and breezy" Etretat he saw in 1876, on Rouen, on Le Havre, like his other pieces, were not the ordinary travel style which the newspaper had expected. He was far less a journalist than a connoisseur, and so was a failure as a reporter, not seeing good copy where it wasn't, not making himself available for what he considered secondrate. The same had been true of the disastrous play *Guy Domville,* in which he had tried "to violate his intrinsic conditions, to make, as it were, a sow's ear out of a silk purse. He tries and he tries and he does what he thinks his coarsest and crudest." It's of no use. That was not what the public wanted. For the *Tribune*, he had reported on the way Verdi conducted his requiem and Strauss conducted his waltzes, talked of the French writers Emile Zola and Ste Beuve. At last, he offered to resign: "if my letters have been 'too good' I

am honestly afraid that they are the poorest I can do." What was wanted was gossip, and he had been writing "magazine rather than newspaper work." (Nozick, 344) Had they always been "too subtle, always too fine—never, never vulgar enough"? He could do no more: they were, he wrote to Whitelaw Reid of the *Tribune*, the very worst he could do. Ah, but worse still, since it was a matter of his most important relation, Henry's reaction to William's

Rudyard Kipling, 1899

Alfred Lord Tennyson

repeated suggestion that he should write more understandably, coherently, obviously, repeated the exact same syndrome. The elliptical author—elusive in the face of demands for straightforwardness—was determined (quite rightly) to treasure his elusiveness.

Why not write, for example, like Rudyard Kipling? James's opinion of Kipling was not a complimentary one. He had, said the Master, gone progressively downward: "he has come steadily from the less simple in subject to the more simple—from the Anglo-Indians to the natives, from the natives to the Tommies, from the Tommies to the quadrupeds . . . a dear little chap. And, *such* an uninteresting mind." (Edel 4, 52) Understandably Kipling destroyed most of James's letters to him.

Another disappointment was Alfred Lord Tennyson. On one weekend, in the country home of Richard Monckton Milnes, Lord Houghton, at dinner, there were Gladstone and Heinrich Schliemann (the discoverer of Troy, Schliemann, knew no Greek until he was 34, and then learned it in six weeks, in St. Petersburg: "*Ce que c'est d'être Allemand!*" (Edel 2, 287). James remarked on the strange simplicity of Tennyson, who talked exclusively of port wine and tobacco, but, as James was astonished to learn, Tennyson had admired one of James's stories and was fully aware of the young novelist. The old poet, however, when asked to read, recited his own "Locksley Hall" solemnly, in a sort of chant not at all Tennysonian. (Nozick, 393)

There were, however, brighter moments. At the Humphrey Wards, in London, he met Matthew Arnold, E.M.Forster, and the bluestocking to end all bluestockings, Violet Paget (a.k.a. Vernon Lee) "She has a prodigious cerebration," James remarked, and at another point, writ-

ing to Gosse, he declared, "She has a mind—almost the only one in Florence." She could discuss, he said, "all things in any language, and understands some, drives her pen, glares through her spectacles and keeps up her courage . . ." (Edel 3, 115, 212)

James's own cerebration was the most obvious thing about him. When T.S. Eliot remarked that he had a mind so fine that no idea could penetrate it, the remark was not altogether pejorative. Gradually, James's works took on titles more and more symbolic: from *Washington Square* to *The Golden Bowl*, from *Portrait of a Lady*, an attempt to construct the story for Minny as if she had gone on living, to *Wings of the Dove,* for which he made notes in the exact year of the death of Fenimore in Venice. Several persons merge here: Kate and Mildred Theory, Minny Temple, towards the making of Milly Theale—whose palazzo in *The Wings of the Dove* (where it is called the Palazzo Leporelli) is modeled on the Palazzo Barbaro, the fifteenth century Gothic building which played host so often to James.

The more colorful English authors James met all the time.(Letters, 79 March 29, 1877 to WJ) Huxley he found "a very genial, comfortable being—yet with none of the noisy & windy geniality of some folks here." In 1867 he met Dickens at Shady Hill, wearing a bright red vest. And once, contemplating a Titian at the National Gallery, he found himself standing next to Algernon Swinburne, (Auto, 569) observing "the largest and most chevelu auburn head I had ever seen perched on a scarcely perceptible body . . . thrilled . . . that I should be admiring Titian in the same breath with Mr. Swinburne."

He found Robert Browning—who often stayed near Katherine Bronson in Venice, in her guest rooms in the Palazzo Giustinian-Recanati or in the Ca'Alvisi, and who was his neighbor at De Vere Gardens in London—"infinitely talkative" (Kaplan, 76) and more than impressive. Browning loved Venice with a passion as great as that of

James, and at his death in the Ca Rezzonico, there was engraved on his plaque his often-quoted statement of the city that remained in his soul. But his funeral in 1889 at Westminster Abbey led James to contemplate "the seriousness of the great human passion."

With Charles Eliot Norton and his wife, Henry went to hear the great John Ruskin lecturing on Greek Myths at University College, and then visited him at Denmark Hill, finding him to be "a man scared back by the grim face of reality into the world of unreason and illusion . . . he wanders . . . without a compass and a guide—or any light save the fitful flashes of his beautiful genius." (Kaplan, 96) Norton had written about Ruskin: "I read to him what you say of Tintoret, which

Above: Plaque for Ca Rezzonico—"Robert Browning died in this Palazzo, December 12, 1889, placed here by Venice. 'Open my heart and you will see/ Graved inside of it Italy.'"

Left: Front of Ca Rezzonico

had greatly pleased me . . . the cordial admiration he felt for your work . . . his warm expression of the good it did him, to find such sympathies & such appreciations, and to know that you were to be added to the little list of those who really, & intelligently & earnestly care for the same things that have touched him most deeply, & influenced his life most powerfully . . . a man of genius very solitary, & with very few friends who care for what he cares for." (Edel 2, 128) Ruskin had said, Norton wrote, that he very much wished that James had been appointed Slade Professor of Fine Arts at Cambridge rather than Sidney Colvin.

As he wrote in his notebook (Notebook, 53), on Sunday, May 19, 1889, with the Nortons, he went also to visit William Morris, where there was Jane, the Pre-Raphaelite's favorite model: "an apparition of fearful and wonderful intensity . . . a tall lean woman in a long dress of some dead purple stuff . . . with a mass of crisp, black hair heaped into great wavy projections on each of her temples, a thin pale face, a pair of strange, sad, deep, dark Swinburnish eyes, with great thick black oblique brows, joined in the middle and tucking themselves away under her hair." (Kaplan,97)

He met George Eliot—whose *Daniel Deronda* and *Middlemarch* he vigorously admired—and was immensely impressed by her. For him, she proved "how few limitations are of necessity implied in the feminine organism." In May of 1869, he wrote to his father about the way she charmed him: "in this vast ugliness resides a most powerful beauty which, in a very few minutes steals forth and charms the mind, so that you end as I ended, in falling in love with her. Yes behold me literally in love with this great horse-faced blue-stocking." She shows "a mingled sagacity and sweetness—a broad hint of a great underlying world of reserve, knowledge, pride and power—a great feminine dignity and character in these massively plain features—a hundred con-flicting shades of consciousness and simpleness . . . Altogether, she has a larger circumference than any woman I have ever seen." (Edel 1, 294-5)

George Eliot Henry James loved paintings—among those he most loved were Haydon's huge canvasses, such as *The Banishment of Aristides*. The James family had all three volumes of his Auto-biography at home: "new, shiningly new, and if he hinted that we might per-haps in some happy future emulate his big bravery there was nothing impossible about it." (Auto, 177) He loved Anthony Van Dyck's *Portrait of Charles I* on horseback, "a thing of infi-

nite beauty," Titian's *Assumption,* and his *Ritratto Virile* in the Pitti Palace, a man in "black clothes, inscrutable, violent expression in his eyes," and (Letters, 30) one great picture at the Dora Palace, Velasquez's portrait of *Innocent X.* He greatly admired—like Ruskin himself—the works of Tintoretto, particularly his rendition of the *Last Supper,* with its strong diagonal line. "It was the whole scene that Tintoret seemed to have beheld in a flash of inspiration intense enough to stamp it ineffaceably on his perception, and it was the whole scene, complete, peculiar, individual, unprecedented, that he committed to canvas with all the vehemence of his talent . . . its long, diagonally-placed table, its dusky spaciousness, its scattered lamp-light and halo-light, its startled, gesticulating figures . . ."(Letters, 26) About the startling and enormous *Crucifixion in the Scuola di San Rocco,* he wrote:

> "The greatest picture it seemed to me as I looked at it I ever saw . . . there is everything in it." (Venice, 115).

Portrait of Pope
Innocent X, *Diego
Velasquez*

James might have agreed with Vasari, who called Tintoretto "the most extraordinary mind that the art of painting has produced." Writing to his father, from the Hotel Barbesi in Venice, on Sept. 17,1869, he claimed that "the grand Titian already trembles, nay, actually sinks, in the scale. There is a grander than he in the terrible Tintoretto—& a greater than either possibly in the sublime Bellini." (21) Speaking of Bellini's *Madonna and Child with Saints Nicholas, Peter, Benedict and Mark* (1488), in its original frame, he enthused: "It seems painted with molten gems, which has been clarified by time, and it is as solemn as it is gorgeous and as simple as it is deep." (Venice, 113)

About the del Piombo painting above the altar in the church of San Giovanni Crisostome—this painter who was trained under Bellini, and influenced by Giorgione, he spoke of being impressed by Mary Magdalen. She looked, he said, like a "dangerous, but most valuable acquaintance." (Venice, 95)

Virgin and Child,
Giovanni Bellini

Madonna
delle Grazie,
*Sebastiano
Luciana Del
Piombo*

The Way it Ended

In 1900, after all the years in London, Henry James settled in Lamb House, in "little restful, red-roofed, uncomplicated Rye." (Edel 5, 35) When young, he had galloped on horseback past Italian shepherds; now, on the cobbled streets of Rye, he went about on bicycle, often in checked black and white trousers, wearing a cloth cap—a far cry from the crimson cape and black top hat he would wear in Italy. Now he had his fat dog, Maximilian the red dachsund, and Tosca, his canary, and his habits. He would go around the sea roads, to the little towns, to Winchelsea to visit the actress Ellen Terry.

He loved his garden, and wrote to his garden lady, Miss Muir McKenzie, about it, and the autumn in Rye: "the tree forms grow in

Left: Henry James at Lamb House, Rye, c. 1907

Below: Lamb House

beauty as they simplify in dress; the grey sky is streaked with vague pink; . . . and the stillness is like the long gulp or catching of breath that precedes . . . a long sob, or other vocal outbreak." (Edel 5, 106)

When, in 1911, he needed to leave behind the depression, "solitude, confinement and immobilization" he had felt in winter-gloomy Rye, he moved back to London. But he could not inhabit his room in his beloved Reform Club and continue writing, given that a female typist was forbidden in the all-male establishment. So he moved to a small place Bosanquet had located for him, on Lawrence Street in Chelsea.

In 1912, alas, he developed shingles, always painful, but enjoyed the company of his nephew and his bride, and the small tasks of shopping. He moved to 21 Carlyle Mansions, in Cheyne Walk in Chelsea, where he had two large rooms, looking out over the long view Whistler had painted in one of his famous *Nocturne*s, of 1871. At a Christmas party at Edmond Gosse's in 1912, he met André Gide, "an interesting Frenchman." Gide's private—not so private—preferences may have appealed to him intellectually, and his work visiting wounded soldiers laid up in St. Bartholomew's hospital must have reminded him of Walt Whitman's like visits. James raised money for

Nocturne: Blue and Silver, *James Abbott McNeill Whistler, 1871*

Belgian refugees, and became the chair of the American Volunteer Motor Ambulance Corps.

For James's 70th birthday, Edith Wharton commissioned a portrait of him by the great painter Sargent. Dissatisfied with it, the painter tore it up, and began again.

At the same time as the portrait, James was given a real golden bowl, a reproduction of a seventeenth-century item, along with Sargent's portrait. Not entirely in jest, when in May of 1914 an enthusiastic suffragette broke the glass covering this portrait and slashed it—without knowing whom it represented—James protested his distress. "I naturally feel very scalped and disfigured." (He never wanted to be seen with reading glasses, and, indignity of indignities, had had all his

teeth removed. But the portrait shows only dignity.)

Edith, who gave the portrait to James, did something else, which was less agreeable for him. She managed at one point to divert some of her own royalties to him, and even raised a subscription for him—provoking in him an understandably great fury when he found it out. When Wharton left England in mid-August of 1912, it was, said James, as if a "whirligig" had departed. But an admirable one: "Long life to her—even at the cost of a shorter one . . . to others." (Kaplan, 562) It was one of the great friendships of literature.

In late October of 1915, James fell sick, and one of his legs collapsed under him. He suffered a stroke on December 2, and gradually became obsessed with the Napoleonic world, dictating orders about the decoration of his imperial palaces and reporting to his brother and sister on his campaigns. As David Lodge describes these hallucinations in his *Author, Author*, "These elaborate fantasies are, in their way, impressive evidence of a still active imagination, like the last salvoes of a holed sinking, but defiant battleship." (Lodge, 19) So the little boy who had remembered the Napoleonic column, refound that world in his memory. And he joined the Old World. In 1915, when he had lived in England for forty years, he was still considered—now during the First World War—an alien, and this, together with his discouragement over America's hesitation to join the war effort, persuaded him. With Gosse as his sponsor, he became a British Subject. On New Year's Day of 1916, he was awarded the Order of Merit, and died on February 18.

He was buried in the Cambridge cemetery by his family, in that James country he had always been part of. Although he is so often quoted as saying, at the end of his life, "Here it comes at last, the distinguished thing," it is perhaps more fitting to remember his saying, "Nothing is my *last word* about anything." (Horne, Letters, 104)

After all, he had found that "It takes one whole life for some persons *dont je suis,* to learn how to live at all." (Edel 5, 165) I think that he never lost that initial "wonder of consciousness in everything," noted in his autobiography (xiv) and that his curiosity remained, living for us even now.

Portrait of
Henry James,
*John Singer
Sargent, 1912*

Chronology

1830	Henry James Senior graduates from Union College
1843	Henry James Senior sails to Europe; on April 15, Henry Jr. is born in New York City
1855	the family sails back to Europe: Liverpool, London, Paris: Henry sees Géricault's *The Raft of the Medusa*, in its "splendour and terror of interest"; they visit Geneva and London, where Henry sees Charles Kean in Shakespeare, Alred Wigan in French melodrama, and Charles Mathews in a Sheridan play
1856	back to Paris, and stay on the rue de Seine; Henry, on the sight of Luxembourg Palace: "Such a stretch of perspective, such an intensity of tone as it offered in those days."
1857	Boulogne-sur-Mer; stays on the rue Neuve Chaussée and in October on the rue Montaigne and then the Grande-Rue: one winter was enough for them all
1858-60	last trip as family to Europe; back to Newport; William studies art with William Morris Hunt and John LaFarge; Henry translates Alfred Musset's *Lorenzaccio* and Prosper Merimée's *Vénus de l'îsle*
1861	William will become a scientist; a severe fire, in which Henry is trapped in a corner, and sprains his back: his illness is always referred to as an "obscure hurt"
1862	joins William in Cambridge boarding house, then in Winthrop Square; makes a "Law school experiment"
1864	the James family moves from Newport to Boston, on Ashburton Place
1866	they live at 20 Quincy St., Cambridge
1867	Henry meets Dickens at Shady Hill
1869	to Europe; Minny dies; Henry meets Paul Joukowsky, who ends up as part of Richard Wagner's entourage
1877	Henry meets John Addington Symonds, who writes about homoeroticism
1878	*Daisy Miller*; meets Julia Duckworth
1880	*Washington Square*
1881	*Portrait of a Lady*
1886	*The Princess Casamassima*; William buys barn and houses at Chocorua Lake
1888	Lizzie Boott dies in Paris; *The Aspern Papers*
1889	meets Georges Du Maurier, Hippolyte Taine; Robert Barrett Browning

	dies
1890	meets Morton Fullerton
1895	*The Figure in the Carpet*; *Guy Domville* is performed
1898	*The Turn of the Screw*
1899	shaves off beard
1900	joins the Reform Club in London
1901	Queen Victoria dies; with Morton Fullerton and Edith Wharton at the Mount; William resigns his professorship
1902	*The Wings of the Dove*
1903	*The Ambassadors*
1904	*The Golden Bowl*
1905	back to New York for a visit
1906	Coburn photographs him at Rye
1906	drives three days with "the avenging angel," Edith Wharton in her speeding Panhard
1907	*The American Scene*; Henry and Hendrik Andersen in Rome; Theodora Bosanquet becomes his secretary; Fullerton confesses the blackmail he is subject to
1908	Fullerton and Edith in the hotel at Charing Cross in London; Henry meets Jocelyn Persse
1909	a bonfire burns almost all the letters he had ever received, and he burns many others, so as not to leave them at "the mercy of any accidents"
January 1910	falls ill
March 1910	William and Alice come to Rye; to Switzerland with William
1910 late June,	in Chocorua, William dies: "my protector, my backer, my authority and my pride."
July 1911	Henry goes back to England
May 1914	he does war work; a suffragette breaks the glass of Sargent's portrait of James and slashes it
1914	last meeting with Edith Wharton; H.G. Wells parodies him in *Boon*
1915	Rupert Brooke dies in the Mediterranean
1915	Applies for British citizenship in June 1915, with Edmund Gosse as his sponsor; in late October falls sick, his leg collapses, and in his mind he enters a Napoleonic world
1916	New Year's Day, he is awarded the Order of Merit
	He dies on February 18; buried in the James family plot in Cambridge, Massachusetts

Bibliography

Davis, Deborah. Strapless: *John Singer Sargent and the Fall of Madame X*. New York: Penguin, 2004.

Edel, Leon. *Henry James* (5 vol). New York: Avon, 1962.
    no. 1. *The Untried Years 1843-1870*.
    no. 2 *The Conquest of London 1870-1882*.
    no. 3 *The Middle Years 1882-1895*.
    no. 4 *The Treacherous Years 1895-1901*.
    no. 5 *The Master 1901-1916*.

James, Henry
——*Autobiography of Henry James*. (Includes *A Small Boy & Others, Notes of a Son & Brother, and The Middle Years*.) Ed. Frederick W. Dupee. Princeton: Princeton University Press, 1983. A
——*Henry James: A Life in Letters*, ed. Philip Horne. New York: Viking, 1999.
——*The Complete Notebooks of Henry James*, ed. Leon Edel. New York: Oxford, 1987. N

Kaplan, Fred. *Henry James: the Imagination of Genius: A Biography*. New York: William Morrow and Co., 1992. K

Lewis, R.W.B. *The Jameses: A Family Narrative*. New York: Doubleday Anchor, 1991.

Lodge, David. *Author, Author*. New York: Viking, 2004.

Lowell, Amy. *Selected Poems*, ed. Honor Moore. New York: Library of America (American Poets Project), 2005.

Menand, Louis. *The Metaphysical Club: A Story of Ideas in America*. New York: Farrar Straus Giroux, 2001. LM

Nozick, Sheldon M. *Henry James: the Young Master*. New York: Random House, 1996.

Carol M. Osborne, *Duveneck: Franck Duveneck & Elizabeth Boott Duveneck*. New York: Owen Gallery, 1996.

Tintner, Adeline R. *The Twentieth-Century World of Henry James: Changes in His Work after 1900*. Baton Rouge: Louisiana State University Press, 2000.

Toíbín, Colm. *The Master*. New York: Scribner's, 2004.

List of Illustrations

List of illustrations (by page number) and photographic acknowledgments. Every effort has been made to contact all copyright holders. The publishers will be happy to correct in future editions any errors or omissions brought to their attention.

ii. (frontispiece) Henry James, John La Farge, 1862. Courtesy of the Century Association, New York, NY.

3. Henry James. By permission of the Houghton Library, Harvard University.

4. Mrs. William James, Mary Margaret James, William James and Henry James in Cambridge, Mass., 1904. By permission of the Houghton Library, Harvard University.

5. Ralph Waldo Emerson, George K. Warren, c. 1870. National Portrait Gallery, Smithsonian Institution/Art Resource, NY.

6. Adjutant (Garth Wilkinson) James and Lt.-Col. Hallowell, July, 1863. By permission of the Houghton Library, Harvard University.

7(t). Franck Duveneck, Henry James, Sr., c. 1880. By permission of the Houghton Library, Harvard University.

7(b). Augustus Saint-Gaudens. William Dean Howells, with Daughter Mildred, 1898. National Portrait Gallery, Washington, DC/Art Resource, NY.

8. Galerie d'Apollon.

9. Henry James, Sr., and Henry James, Jr, 1830. Photograph by Matthew Brady. By permission of the Houghton Library, Harvard University.

10(t). The Vendôme Column, c. 1870. Musée de la Ville de Paris, Musée Carnavalet, Paris. Snark/Art Resource, NY.

10(b). Théodore Géricault, The Raft of the Medusa. 1819. Louvre. Réunion des Musées Nationaux/Art Resource, NY.

11(t). William James, aged 19. By permission of the Houghton Library, Harvard University.

11(b). Charles Kean.

12(t). View of Boulogne.

12(b). William James in Geneva, 1859-60. By permission of the Houghton Library, Harvard University.

13. John La Farge, Peacocks and Peonies I, 1882. Smithsonian American Art Museum, Washington, D.C./Art Resource, NY.

14(t). Mary James, c. 1875. By permission of the Houghton Library, Harvard University.

14(b). *William James in the Garden at Lamb House,* Rye, East Susex, 1908. By permission of the Houghton Library, Harvard University.

15. Ilya Repin, *Portrait of Ivan Turgenev.* Galleria Statale Tretiakov, Moscow/Art Resource, N.Y.

16. Henry James, March, 1890. Elliott and Fry. By permission of the Houghton Library, Harvard University.

17. Alice Boughton. *Photograph of Henry James*, 1906. National Portrait Gallery, Smithsonian Institution/Art Resource, NY.

18. Henry James in London.

19. Henry James in the Garden at Lamb House, Rye, East Sussex, c. 1900. By permission of the Houghton Library, Harvard University.

20(t). *Henry James at his Desk in the Garden House.* By permission of the Houghton Library, Harvard University.

20(b). Henry James at Lamb House

21(t). Trafalgar Square, London

21(b). De Vere Gardens, London.

22(t). *Henry and William in Rye*, 1901. By permission of the Houghton Library, Harvard University.

22(b). *Henry James*, Rome, 1899. By permission of the Houghton Library, Harvard University.

24. *Henry James*, from pencil sketch by Sargent.

25. John Singer Sargent, *Vernon Lee*, 1881. Tate Gallery, London/Art Resource, NY.

26. Henry James, 1882.

27. Alice Boughton, *William James,* 1907. By permission of the Houghton Library, Harvard University.

28. William Glackens, *Garden at 110 rue du Bac*, 1929. Owens Gallery, NY.

29. Torquay.

30. Boston Commons.

32(t). Piazza San Marco, Venice. Author photograph.

32(l). No. 4161 Riva degli Schiavoni, Venice. Author photograph.

32(r). Wall sign, Riva Schiavoni, Venice. Author photograph.

33(t). Cafe Florian, Venice. Author photograph.

33(b). Gran Caffe Quadri, Venice. Author photograph.

34. Jacques-Emile Blanche. *Marcel Proust*, 1893. Beinecke Library, Yale University, New Haven, CT.

35, 36. Palazzo Barbaro, Venice. Author photographs.

37. Reform Club, London.

39(t). Frank Edwin Larson, *Portrait of Mark Twain.* National Porgtrait Gallery, Smithsonian Institution/Art Resource, NY

39(b). Julia Margaret Cameron, *photograph of Mrs. Julia Duckworth*, 1867. Art Resource, NY.

41. Walter Tittle, *Portrait of Joseph Conrad.* National Portrait Gallery/Art Resource, NY.

42(t). *Marcel Proust.* The Newberry Library, Chicago, IL.

42(b). W. Warman. Portrait of Charles Dickens. The Pierpont Morgan Library/Art Resource, NY.

43. Eugene Carrière. *Alphonse Daudet and his daughter Edmée.* 1890. Musée d'Orsay/Art Resource, NY.

44. *George Sand.* Herzog-Anton-Ulrich-Museum, Braunschweig, Germany/Art Resource, NY.

45(t). *Paul Zoukovskye, 1875.* By permission of the Houghton Library, Harvard University.

45(b). Eugène Giraud. *Portrait of Gustave Flaubert*, 1856. Chateaux de Versailles et de Trianon, Versailles, France. Réunion des Musées Nationaux/Art Resource, NY

46. *Minny Temple, at 16*, 1868. By permission of the Houghton Library, Harvard University.

47. p. 29François-Nicolas Feyen-Perrin, *Portrait of Guy de Maupassant.* Chateaux de Versailles et de Trianon, Versailles, France. Réunion des Musées Nationaux/Art Resource, N.Y.

48. *Edith Wharton.* Library, Yale University, New Haven, CT.

49. *Teddy Wharton*, 1896. Beinecke Library, Yale University, New Haven, CT.

51. *Morton Fullerton.* Photograph. Beinecke Library, Yale University, New Haven, Ct

53. *The Mount.* Beinecke Library, Yale University, New Haven, CT.

54. Walter Berry at the Mount, c. 1911. Beinecke Library, Yale University, New Haven, CT

55. *Edith Wharton with Two Dogs*, c. 1884. Library, Yale University, New Haven, CT.

56. *Henry James, Howard Henry Sturgis, and the Boits, Vallombrosa*, 1907. By permission of the Houghton Library, Harvard University.

58. *Minny Temple, 1869.* By permission of the Houghton Library, Harvard University.

60(t). *Alice James, June, 1870.* . By permission of the Houghton Library, Harvard University.

60(b). *Elizabeth Boott.* By permission of the Houghton Library, Harvard University.

61. *Alice James in Kensington, June 1891*, by Katherine Loring. By permission of the Houghton Library, Harvard University.

62. *Constance Fenimore Woolson.* By permission of the Houghton Library, Harvard University.

63. Villa Brichieri-Colombi, Bellosguardo (*top*) and Villa Castellai, Bellosguardo (*bottom*).

64(t). Elizabeth Boott Duveneck, *Pink Roses in a Vase*, 1883. Dedicated to Alice James. Courtesy of the Owens Gallery, NY.

64(b). *Photo of Frank Duveneck in Venice*, 1974. Courtesy of the Owens Gallery.

65. James Abbott McNeill Whistler, *Harmony in Blue and Silver: Trouville*, 1845. Isabella Stewart Gardner Museum, Boston/Art Resource, NY.

66. William Wetmore Story, *The Libyan Sibyl*, 1868. National Museum of American Art, Washington, D.C./Art Resource, NY.

67. John Ruskin, *Self-Portrait in Blue Neckcloth.* The Pierpont Morgan Library, N.Y./Art Resource, NY.

69. Fanny Kemble.

71. Henri de Toulouse-Lautrec, *Oscar Wilde*, 1895. Conrad H. Lester Collection, N.Y. /Art Resource, NY.

72. Hendrik Andersen, *Portrait bust of Henry James,* Rome/Art Resource, NY.

74. Alice Boughton. *Photograph of Henry James*, c. 1906.

76. Eugène Delacroix, *Self-portrait.* Louvre, Paris/Art Resource, NY.

77. Max Beerbohm, *Caricature of John Singer Sargent*, 1910. Tate Gallery/Art Resource, NY.

78. John Singer Sargent. *Study of Mme Gautreau,* ca. 1884. Tate Gallery, London/Art Resource, NY

79. Curtis Doorbell, Palazzo Barbaro, Venice. Author photograph.

80(t). Statue of Wagner in Venice. Author photograph.

80(b). James Abbot McNeill Whistler, *Robert, Comte de Montesquiou-Fezensac.* Frick Collection, NY.

81. Max Beerbohm, *Oscar Wilde,* 1882. Tate Gallery, London/Art Resource, NY.

83. *Sarah Bernhardt as Phèdre*. Photograph. Paul Nadar Archives, Paris.

84. Philip Burne-Jones, *Rudyard Kipling.* 1899. National Portrait Gallery/Art Resource, NY.

85. Julia Margaret Cameron, photo of Alfred Lord Tennyson. Art Resouce, NY.

86. Wall Sign, Fondamenta Barbaro, Venice. Author photograph.

87(t). Plaque at Ca Rezzonico for Robert Browning, Venice. Author photograph.

87(b). Ca Rezzonico, front, Venice. Author photograph.

89. *George Eliot*, Art Resource, NY.

90. Diego Velasquez, *Portrait of Pope Innocent X.* Galleria Doria Pamphilii, Rome. Alinari/Art Resource, NY.

91(t). Giovanni Bellini, *The Virgin with the Child*, Chiesa di Santa Maria Gloriosa dei Frati; Sacristy, Venice/Art Resource, NY.

91(b). Sebastiano Luciana Del Piombo *Madonna delle Grazie Sanctuary*. Church of San Giovanni Crisostomo, Venice/Art Resource, NY.

92. Henry James in Wicker Chair at Lamb House, Rye, c. 1907. By permission of the Houghton Library, Harvard University.

93. Lamb House, Rye. By permission of the Houghton Library, Harvard University.

94. James Abbott McNeill Whistler, *Nocturne: Blue and Silver*, 1871. Tate Gallery, London/Art Resource, N.Y.

95(t). *André Gide with Marc Allegret, playing chess*, 1947. Les Albums photographiques.

95(b). Frank E. Pearsall, *Photograph of Walt Whitman*, 1872. Art Resource, NY.

96. John Singer Sargent, *Portrait of Henry James*, 1912. By permission of the Houghton Library, Harvard University.